Cannon Boy Of The Alamo

By R.L. Templeton

Copyright 1975 by R.L. Templeton

*Published In The United States Of America
By Nortex Press, Quanah, Texas*

All Rights Reserved

ISBN 0-89015-085-0

This book is dedicated
to every boy that loved a dog
and was loved by a dog.

THE ALAMO TODAY

(Courtesy the San Antonio Chamber of Commerce)

**Cannon Boy
Of The
Alamo**

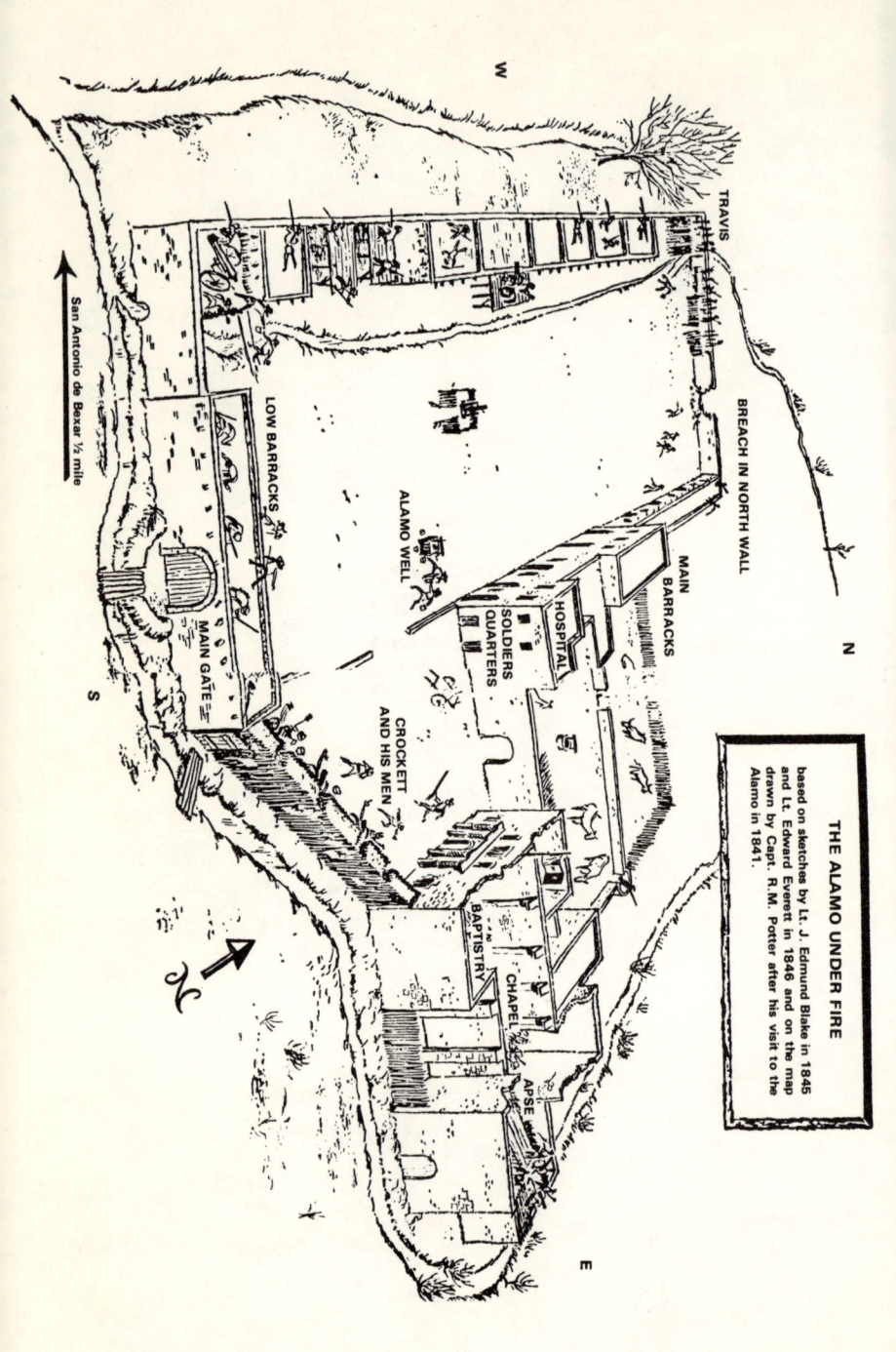

INTRODUCTION

Billy King, the 15-year-old unshaven boy from Gonzales, Texas, the youngest man to die in the Alamo when it fell on March 6, 1836, cried out to me to tell his story. He has no grave. Like the other 182 men who died in the Alamo, his body was burned in the patio, just east of the present Chapel that we think of as the Alamo.

The story of Billy King is written so that his heroism and courage may be "tasted" and appreciated, so that other 15-year-olds may know that Texas' youngest hero was a freckle-faced age 15, and that he went to war with his dog, Comanche, and without a gun.

Billy King entered the Alamo on March 1st, 1836, six days before it fell, he entered at night, riding through Mexican patrols, at times carrying his dog on his saddle beside him. Ready to fight, even though he had no gun.

Read Billy King's story. Feel what it was like to die at age 15 in the Alamo, beside Crockett, Bowie, Travis, and grizzled old cannoneer Sergeant William Ward.

But don't forget his Indian dog, Comanche, who slept with his master and died at Billy King's side, like a faithful dog should.

I am saddened that Texas' youngest hero's story has remained thus far untold, his young courage as silent as the Alamo's hallowed walls.

Lee Templeton

CHAPTER I

"Down Comanche!" Billy shouted at his wolf-like Indian dog, before Comanche could raise his hackles and start racing toward the on-coming horsemen. "You stay right where you are." He patted his dog and pointed to the spot by the wood-pile where he wanted his dog to wait. "Horsemen coming, Pa!" Billy turned and shouted at his father, John King, who already had heard the horses and was stepping out of the barn in anxious long strides, shading his eyes from the late-evening sun with his hand.

"It looks like Captain Kimball and the Volunteers from Gonzales." John King spoke to Billy as the father placed his arm around his tall, slender son.

The father and son stood silently in the middle of the road that rambled through the oak-covered hills between Gonzales and San Antonio.

Captain Kimball reigned in his horse through the white road-dust and held up his hand for the men behind him to stop.

"Howdy, John," Captain Kimball shouted as he turned his huge, white horse and headed through the opened gate toward the long, wooden hitching rack in front of the King cabin.

Billy King ran forward and took Captain Kimball's reins after he dismounted from his white horse, Mad Hatter. Captain Kimball handed the reins to Billy, who quickly looped the reins over the hitching rack and reached for the other reins as two dozen other horsemen galloped up amidst a shower of dust.

John King leaned his hay fork against the hitching rack and walked toward Captain Kimball in swift, happy steps. "Glad to see you, George." John King stepped forward with his hand outstretched to shake hands with Captain Kimball. "Where ya headed in such a hurry at this late hour?" King asked.

Captain Kimball took off his gloves and shook hands, then swatted at the dust along his britches and around his shoulders. He turned and studied his dust-covered soldiers. "We're on our way to San Antonio to relieve the garrison in the Alamo."

"It looks like you brought half the men in Gonzales." John King began walking down the line as the men dismounted at the long hitching rack, shaking hands with Freeman Day, William Fishbaugh, and Johnny Garvin. Then he patted Galba Fuqua, a slight boy, sixteen years old with the thin shoulders and long nose of his Jewish ancestry. He slapped Galba on the shoulders, splattering dust off his buckskin jacket.

John King turned to Captain Kimball. "It looks like you've got half the men and all the boys." He grinned as he looked at the young faces of the men climbing off their horses and hitching their reins to the hitching rack.

"Yeah, John," Captain Kimball stuck his gloves inside his belt, "we had to take a few July colts. We're taking every able-bodied man that wants to help us relieve Colonel Travis' garrison in the Alamo."

"Can I go, Pa? Can I go?" Billy King dropped the reins he was fastening to the hitching post at the front porch and ran to his father.

John King shook his head and patted his fifteen-year-old son gently on the shoulder. "Naw, Son, you can't go. Captain Kimball wouldn't take a fifteen-year-old."

"But Pa, I'm big an' I'm able-bodied," Billy pleaded.

John King shook his head and laughed. "You're able-bodied alright, but you lack a lot being a man."

"But, Pa, I'm bigger'n Galba Fuqua." Billy pointed at

Galba, who was walking around bow-legged, trying to get accustomed to being on the ground instead of up on a horse's back.

John King shook his head. "Billy, you're just barely fifteen. You ain't killed but one bear in your life." He laughed and motioned for Billy to start watering the horses at the horse trough. He turned to Captain Kimball. "George, it looks like your horses have put in a day's work. Can't you come in and rest a spell?"

"Thank you, John. We'd like to spend the night if it wouldn't be too much trouble."

"No trouble at all." John King motioned Captain Kimball toward the narrow wooden door of his two-room log cabin. Mrs. King stood just outside the doorway, rubbing flour off her hands onto a white apron. Her belly was big with child. There was a nervous worry in her eyes, shifting from her husband to her son, then to Captain Kimball.

"I was just baking corn pone. I see I'll need to put a few more pans in the oven." Mrs. King stepped aside and nodded courteously at Captain Kimball as his cleated leather boots clomped across the wooden transom of the cabin door.

"Martha, you fix Captain Kimball a drink and get some towels out to this here wash basin so these men can wash the road dust off their faces," John King placed his hand on Billy's shoulder, "while me and Billy get some hay for these horses. Looks like we're gonna have company tonight."

Billy King walked with his head down, even though he felt his father's hand on his shoulder. At the barn door, he turned to his father. "Pa, when am I ever gonna be a man?" Billy stood outside the open barn door, turning and watching the twenty-four men with Captain Kimball unsaddling their horses and staking them out in the tall grass under the oak trees between the cabin and the gate.

John King walked into the barn shaking his head, pulling the wooden two-wheel cart toward the hay rack. "The Lord will tell you, Son." John King backed the hay cart snuggly against the hay rack. "The Lord will tell you when you're ready."

Billy began forking huge forks-full of hay onto the hay cart. "But I am a man, Pa. I do a man's work. I plowed that north field and sowed it in oats, and I sythed it, and I hauled it in and I stacked it in this barn," Billy argued.

"Doin' a man's work don't mean you can do a man's fightin'."

"But Pa, this is my chance. This is my chance to prove I'm a man." Billy was putting two forks-full of hay in the wagon for every fork-full that his father tossed in the wagon.

Billy lay down his fork and jumped on the hay wagon and tromped the hay down, then climbed back on the hay rack and began forking hay like it was fixing to rain.

When the hay was piled high, Billy turned to his pa. "See there, Pa? I forked twice as much hay as you did." His father was still bent over, slowly pitching forksful of hay at the top of the wagon. Billy touched his father on the shoulder. His father raised up slowly and stared at him. "Can I, Pa? Can I go?"

John King pulled a ragged kerchief with holes along its edges out of his pocket and wiped his brow. He set his jaws firmly and shook his head at Billy. "No, Son, you can't go." Then he reached out and placed his leathery hand on his son's shoulder. "And I won't hear any more of this, you hear?"

"But Pa, Captain Kimball's gonna ask for somebody from this house. He's gonna ask for an able-bodied man."

"Yes, I know." John King stuck his hay fork into the hay in the wagon. "When that call comes, I'll be the one to answer it. I'm the man of the house. It's my duty to defend my family."

Billy threw his fork on the ground in disgust and slowly

helped his father raise the cart tongue into the air and begin tugging it out of the barn.

Once they were outside the barn, two men ran from the staked horses to help them pull the cart. They slowly made the rounds of all twenty-five staked horses, tossing out two forksful of hay to each horse. When the wagon was empty, they returned it to the barn.

Billy walked behind his father toward the house, walking slowly with his head down, avoiding the eyes of the twenty-four soldiers laughing and joking around two campfires. Billy stole a glance at the men just before he went into the house, watching them slowly turn a side of deer in the coals of two fires. The deep belly laughs and the shouting, the crackles of roasting deer sounded like they were having a lot of fun. Billy wanted to go join them and lay his blanket down by the fire and sit on the blanket with a rifle cradled in his arms, and laugh and joke and watch the deer slowly broil, and sleep on the ground, between the fire and his rifle. That would be living like a man.

When Billy and his father walked into the house, Captain Kimball was talking to Martha King.

"Martha, you're not gonna take very kindly to me askin' you to give up one of your menfolks to go and help relieve the Alamo, are you?"

Martha was leaning over the fireplace turning hoecakes in a huge castiron skillet.

She raised slowly, and the wooden spoon in her hand trembled. She had put one hand on her hip as she spoke to Captain Kimball. "You're not gonna take my John?"

"I have to ask for an able-bodied man." Captain Kimball raised the huge clay coffee cup in both hands, blew on it for an instant, then brought it to his lips for a sip.

"But I have only John and Billy and all these little ones and I'm . . ." She looked down at her swollen belly.

John King lifted a yellow clay coffee cup out of the cupboard and set it on the table. He turned to Captain

Kimball. "I'm your able-bodied man." He banged the coffee cup on the table. He stared at Captain Kimball. Then he turned his gaze toward Martha. "And I'll have a little rum in my coffee tonight." He pointed at his coffee cup as he looked at his wife. "When a man is called to serve his country, the least he can do is celebrate."

Martha lifted the fat-bottomed coffeepot off the edge of the fireplace and brought it to the table. She filled her husband's cup half full of coffee. She set the coffeepot back on the edge of the fireplace. She pulled back the calico curtains of her cupboard and pulled out a clay jug. She finished filling her husband's coffee cup with dark rum.

Billy pushed his bench closer to the table. "Mama, could I have some coffee, too?"

"It'll just keep you awake," John King growled. Captain Kimball eyed the father and son militarily.

Billy was looking at his empty cup, fingering it lightly. Finally he picked the cup up and held it up in the air and looked at his mother. "Mama, can I have a cup of coffee with a little rum in it?"

Martha nodded her head at her son. "You're old enough for coffee, Billy boy, but not for rum." She picked up the coffeepot and started toward the table.

"Billy wants to be a man." John King raised his coffee cup and sipped his rummed coffee. "He wants to stand in my place in Captain Kimball's Gonzales Volunteers."

Martha dropped the coffeepot. She stared at her son with deep unblinking eyes.

John King grabbed the coffeepot off the stone floor. When he set the coffeepot on the table, Martha covered her eyes with her arm and turned away. "Not my Billy." She cried, shaking and sobbing.

John King walked around the table and put his arms around his wife and pulled her against him. "Now, now, Martha, one of us has to go." He patted his wife gently on the back.

Billy got up slowly from the table, turning his head, looking at his father as he walked toward his mother. He got down on his knees in front of his mother. He took his mother's hands in his. He held her hands to his lips and kissed each hand. He lowered her hands slowly and studied his mother's warm blue eyes.

"Mama, I wanna go."

"Oh no!" Martha King grabbed her son around the neck and pulled his head against her bosom. "Oh no, I can't let you go. I can't let you go. You'll not come back."

Billy grabbed his mother's fast moving hands again and kissed them again. "Mama, you need Daddy and Daddy needs you, and my little sisters, they need Daddy." Billy slowly pulled his mother's hands apart and stared at her swollen belly. "Maybe that little feller'll be a boy, a little boy to take my place."

Martha shook her head and shut her eyes and pulled her son's head against her chest.

Captain Kimball rose slowly from the table, pushing the cane-bottom chair back noisily as he rose. "I think I'd better go." Captain Kimball stared at the mother clinging to her son. "I'd better see about my men."

Martha King opened her eyes and rose to her feet and held one hand out to Captain Kimball. "Oh no, don't go. Don't go and leave me to decide . . . between my husband and my son."

Billy King snapped his fingers. "Mama, I tell you what let's do. Let's spin a bottle."

"Do what?" John King asked as he set his coffee cup down with a bang.

"Let's spin a bottle, and the one it points at will be the one that goes. That's the way to let the Lord decide."

John King was silently studying his empty coffee cup.

"Pa, you said the Lord would tell me when I was a man. Let's spin a bottle and see if he picks me as the man to go."

John King rose slowly from the table. He held his hand out toward Captain Kimball for a a handshake. "Captain Kimball, Sir, I'm your man. John King will be ready at daylight."

The two men shook hands, and Captain Kimball nodded his head at Martha and Billy. He was at the door when John King spoke again.

"Oh, say, there's one other thing. I don't suppose you have an extra gun, do you, Captain? We have only one gun in this household, and I hate to take away the only protection my family has."

Captain Kimball stopped at the door and turned. "No, I'm afraid we don't have an extra gun. In fact, we already have one man without a gun, only a pistol. We're powerfully short of arms and ammunition, too. We're hopin' to pick up a gun between here and San Antonio."

"If I carried away our gun, my family would have nothing to provide deer or turkey, or to protect them from Indians."

Billy ran to his father and held both hands out in entreaty. "Pa, let me go. I don't need a gun. Maybe they have a cannon there. Maybe they'll let me shoot a cannon."

"You wouldn't take a young man without a gun, would you?" John King studied Captain Kimball with a sly grin.

Captain Kimball eyed tall, thin Billy King. "Well, I understand there's either twelve or fourteen cannons in the Alamo. They could always use a young man that's handy with a ramrod."

"If you'll take my Billy without a gun, I might let him go." Martha King summoned a prayerful smile.

"Can I go, Pa? Can I go? Billy pleaded.

John King nodded his head. He walked over and put his arms around Martha King's shoulder to comfort and sustain her. He raised his head and stared over his wife's shoulder at Captain Kimball. "No one in the King family even ran from a fight. I'm letting my son go." John King paused and touched his cheek to his wife's hair. "But I'm not saying I won't catch you before you get to the Alamo."

Martha King began shaking and sobbing as Captain Kimball opened the door behind him.

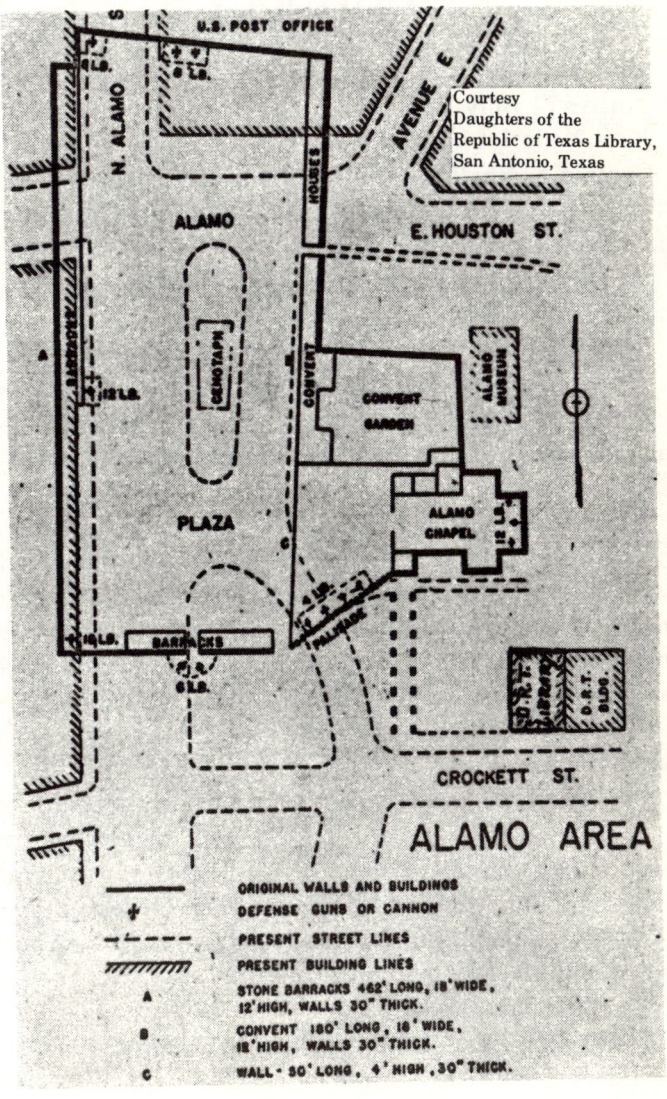

CHAPTER II

"Pa, can I go join 'em now? Do I have to wait 'til tomorrow?" Billy asked his pa.

John King looked over his shoulder at Martha.

Captain Kimball saluted John King, Martha King, and Billy King. Then he stepped out the door quietly, letting the wooden door latch down slowly, quietly.

"Must you go so soon?" Martha held her hands out as she turned to Billy.

"I wanna join them now, tonight."

"But you haven't had your supper. And you have your bed. Where would you sleep?" Martha lowered her hands knowing the boy wanting to go, wouldn't come to her. She wondered if he ever would again.

"Mama, that's what I wanna do. I wanna go out there and spread my blanket on the ground beside them soldiers. I wanna eat roast deer. I wanna share the cold ground and the smoke from the campfire. I want to be one of the men on the way to relieve the Alamo garrison."

Martha shook her head gently with misgiving. "Can't you wait 'til tomorrow?"

Billy shook his head. "I want to be a man on the way to the Alamo. I want to be out there with them tonight."

Martha's eyes pleaded and begged. Her eyes said she wanted her son to spend this last night as close to her as she could hold him. Billy folded his arms across his chest and outstared his pleading mother.

Martha let her face break into a sad but prideful smile. She walked over and placed a hand on each of Billy's shoulders. "My little cannon boy." She slapped him on each shoulder. "I'll have to get you two blankets and an oil cloth. I'll have to fill your saddlebag full of bread and sausage. I'll have to get a water jug and fill it full of sweet milk."

Billy held up his hand. "Ma, just fill it full of water. I'm not going to be drinking milk out there in front of all those men."

Martha King nodded her head slowly, trying to understand, trying to see that her son had grown up. She rushed away to pack his blankets and his saddlebag.

Billy turned to his father. "Pa, can I ask you one thing?"

"Yeah." John King stood with his arms folded across his chest disapprovingly. "You can ask."

"Pa, I know I can't take the gun when I ride off tomorrow, but can I just take it out there and sleep with it tonight?"

"What!"

"I won't be no soldier, Pa, if I walk out there with just my blankets and my saddlebag."

"But you can't take the gun."

"But, Pa, could I just borrow it for tonight? Then when we get ready to ride away tomorrow, you can take it away from me. You can take it away just before we ride away. I'd feel so much better if you'd just let me borrow it for tonight."

John King walked over to the gun rack on the mantle above the fireplace and lifted the rifle off its hooks. He examined it closely for dust. He blew on it and rubbed away some dust. He held the rifle in one hand and lifted the powder horn and shot bag off their hooks above the fireplace with his other hand. He handed them to Billy. "A rifle's no good without a powder horn and shot bag."

"Thanks, Pa." Billy had his hands full, and all he could do was lean his head over and pat it gently against his father's broad shoulders. He raised his head proudly and stared at his pa for a long, thoughtful instant. Then he said, "Thanks, Pa, for letting me be a man."

Billy hefted the filled saddlebag and laid it over his shoulder. His mother handed him the long two-blanket bedroll. He put it on the other shoulder. His father handed him the shot bag and the powder horn. He held them in one hand with their long leather shoulder straps. He took the rifle from his father with his other hand. He nodded at his father as he walked to the door, then he stood staring at the door latch. He tried to open the door with the hand that held the shot bag and the powder horn, but the latch wouldn't rise. He turned and grinned at his father, as he lifted the rifle barrel and tried to use the barrel to raise the door latch, but it wouldn't raise. Billy glanced around at his mother with her hands clasped together. Then he looked at his father, who was leaning with one hand against the wall, smiling at Billy's problem with the door.

"See, you can't even get through a door with your gear," John King laughed.

Billy raised his left foot and kicked the latch, but the door still didn't open. Billy lowered his foot slowly and started to set the shot bag and powder horn down.

Martha King stepped forward with an understanding smile. "Here, Son, let me hold the door for you."

Billy nodded at his mother, thanking her as his rifle and powder horn banged against the door facing as he stepped out into the cold, brisk February night.

Martha stood in the doorway, watching her son stop and hump his gear on his shoulders as he tramped toward the farthest campfire.

His father's big, broad-brimmed black hat slid down lower over his forehead with each step. Billy stopped and shook his head, trying to push the big black hat back on his head to keep it from falling down over his eyes. He had to stop and raise his rifle to push the hat back in its proper place. He walked slowly around to the far side of the fartherest campfire, stepping slowly and gingerly over the quiet blanket-covered men huddled close together around the warming campfire. Billy found an empty space on the far western side of the campfire. He dropped his blanket roll, then shouldered down his shot bag. He shut his eyes as he made a loud racket separating the powder horn from the shot bag, setting them on the ground. As he laid his rifle on the ground beside his blanket roll, a man rose in the bedroll next to him. The man reached out his hand and jerked Billy's britches leg.

"John, you didn't need to join us till tomorrow. We won't be leaving till daylight."

Billy felt his father's black hat sliding down over his eyes. He reached up and pushed it back on his head. "I'm not John; I'm Billy." Billy got down on his hands and knees and began untying his blanket roll and spreading it out on the grass.

The man beside him reached up and pulled off Billy's black hat. He held the hat in his hands for a long, thoughtful instant as he studied Billy's young face in the firelight. He looked at the hat for a second, then handed it back to Billy.

"I'm sorry, Son." The man pulled the blanket back up over his shoulder. "I thought you was John King joinin' us a little early."

Billy jerked the hat and stuck it on his head so quickly that it came down over his face almost to his nose. He jerked the hat off quickly and laid it on the grass beside the rifle. He stayed on his knees, unrolling his blanket bedroll. "I'm Billy G. King. I'm taking my pa's place."

"Oh?" The man raised up on one arm, staring at Billy.

"We got three little ones, and Ma's expectin' another one. That's why I took my pa's place."

"Oh, I see." The man beside Billy rose to his hands and knees and folded his hands across his legs, studying the young man as Billy unrolled his blankets and spread them evenly on the ground. "You look a mite young to me. I don't expect Colonel Travis will accept the likes of you, and the Lord knows he needs all the men he can get."

"How would you know?" Billy slapped the top of his blanket roll.

"How would I know!" the man beside Billy laughed. "I'm John W. Smith. I'm the messenger Colonel Travis sent from the Alamo."

Billy sat on his hands and knees staring at the red-headed man. "You from the Alamo?"

"I'm a carpenter from San Antonio. I was there when General Santa Anna and his troupers rode into town. I helped herd thirty head of beef into the Alamo, and I helped carry in forty sacks of corn, so we'd have some groceries."

"But if you were there," Billy held his hand up, "why are you here?" Billy pointed to the men sleeping on the ground.

John Smith sighed, and then a smile grew on his lips. "They ain't but a hundred and fifty men in the Alamo, and we need a little help. I was sent to Gonzales to ask every able-bodied man to come to the relief of the Alamo."

"Are there many of them? Are there many of the Mexican soldiers?" Billy asked.

"It 'peared to me like they was quite a few of 'em."

"How many?"

"Aw, it looked like the biggest herd of cows I ever saw. Maybe three or four thousand of 'em."

Billy looked around at the blanket-covered men around the two campfires. He blinked and looked at John Smith. "I make twenty-six."

John Smith nodded and lay back on his blanket.

Billy lay down on his blanket and stared through the naked oak limbs at the night sky. He suddenly felt very lonesome. Then he thought of the words John Smith used, "Biggest herd of cows I ever saw." Billy smiled into the night sky and lay down on his blankets, wondering if he would be allowed to shoot a cannon at that big herd of cows.

Then Billy saw a pretty star in the sky, so bright and shiny, so pure and clean. He thought of Amy Anderson. He had to see her before he left. He glanced around at the sleeping men, then he looked toward the barn. He wondered if he could take a horse and ride over to the Anderson place.

The Anderson place was on the road to San Antonio, only two miles down the road. Billy thought of how proud and military he would look as he rode by. Then suddenly he remembered—no rifle. He would have to ride by without a rifle. A man going to war with no gun. He wondered if Captain Kimball would let him stop and talk to Amy as they rode by. At least he could wave at her.

The ground felt suddenly hard and cold, and the thoughts of Amy were warm and soft as Billy pulled his blankets around him.

John Smith, the man next to Billy, kicked him gently and spoke. "You can call me what they do in San Antonio."

"What's that?" Billy asked.

"In San Antonio, they point to my red hair and call me El Colorado."

Billy thought of the carpenter who had left his home in San Antonio to go to the Alamo. And now he had come to Gonzales for volunteers. He was not returning to his home. He was heading back to the Alamo, to guide them through the Mexican lines.

Billy wondered what it was going to be like when they got to San Antonio, and looked through the Mexican lines at the white walls of the Alamo.

Billy wondered if he would see any cannons sticking through the walls of the Alamo.

CHAPTER III

Billy felt the horses stomping and heard them nickering. Then he smelled bacon frying in the skillet. He heard men talking, and suddenly he remembered how cold he was. He reached outside his blanket and felt of the frosted grass. Suddenly he was awake. He remembered. It was late February, 1836. He was in the Texas army. That's why he was so cold and sleepy. That's why there were so many horses nickering and stomping.

He rolled out of his blankets and felt of the white frost on the grass. No wonder he got so cold. He reached down and felt of his toes to see if they were too frozen to move. They moved. He felt them move in his black stockings as he slid on his boots.

It wasn't good daylight. There were only gray bars in the east. Yet, he could see, smell, and hear bacon frying in the huge three-legged skillet in the edge of the campfire below his bed.

Billy wiped the frost off the barrel of his father's gun. He wiped it clean and dry quickly, then gathered up the shot bag and powder horn and trotted to the cabin with the gun, so he could return it to the mantle over the fireplace before it got light enough for the men to see him returning his pa's gun.

When Billy opened the door, he spied his mother sitting on the stone seat at the edge of the fireplace. She wasn't cooking or doing anything. She still had on her nightgown. She just sat there looking at coals at the edge of the fireplace, staring at the fire. She looked like she might have been there all night.

When Billy pushed the door open wide, his mother

turned with a gasp. "Oh Billy, you scared me." She rose and held her arms out to Billy, but Billy walked right by her and hung the rifle on the mantle of the fireplace. Then he hung the leather shot bag and the powder horn on their hooks above the fireplace.

Billy turned and took his mother's hands. "Gee, Ma," Billy felt of his mother's hands, "your hands feel cold." He felt of her shoulders. Then he looked at her. "Ma, you feel cold all over, like you ain't even been in bed."

Martha King bit her lip and shook her head. "I couldn't sleep."

"I didn't sleep much, either," Billy smiled as he patted his mother on the shoulder and comforted her. "I gotta put a saddle and bridle on ole Alexander and get him ready for the road."

"It's nice to have your own horse, isn't it, Son?" Martha followed Billy to the rear of the house. Billy stood at the back door.

"Yeah, ole Alexander ain't much horse, but he's mine. I know when I was chopping cotton, and picking cotton, and hauling wheat and oats and rye to the mill, and spending the night in the mill waiting to get it ground, then hauling it back, hauling grain for Mr. Anderson and all our neighbors, it seemed like I never was going to get that horse paid for."

"Well, I'm glad you bought a horse instead of a gun." His mother stood between the door and Billy.

Billy glanced back at his father's gun hanging over the fireplace. "Yeah, but I wish I had a gun today. It's gonna be embarrassing being in the Army and having no gun."

"Well, I'm not embarrassed that you are riding off without a gun." She held Billy's hand as he walked through the door and out toward the barn. "I don't think I could stand it if you were to ride away with a gun in your arm."

Billy tossed a disagreeing wave at his mother and headed for the barn and his horse.

Alexander was so nervous and jumpy that he grabbed the bit in his teeth and almost helped Billy put the bridle over his ears. He turned and nudged Billy as Billy spread the saddleblanket and put the saddle on top of it. Alexander was in a hurry this morning. He wanted to get out there under the oak trees where all the other horses were. Billy led him over to the horse trough for a drink, then to the hitching rack.

Alexander began to nicker and paw and scratch and bite the horses around him at the hitching rack. Billy patted him on the butt as he walked away, figuring this was Alexander's way of telling the others that this was his place.

Billy carried his saddlebag and his blanket roll to the hitching rack and tied them on Alexander just behind the saddle. Alexander was nodding his head. Billy smiled at how ole Alexander was telling him how happy he was with all the horse company he suddenly had.

Billy walked down to the campfire with Poe Allen and his little brother, Jim Allen. He stood in line for a tin plate of scrambled eggs and bacon, and a cup of coffee. Billy sniffed of the thick slice of home-made bread that was dropped on top of the bacon and eggs. The bread came from his mother's oven, the eggs came from their chickenhouse, and the bacon came from their smokehouse. The only food the Army furnished was the coffee, but it looked like the army did furnish the coffee cup and the plate he ate off of.

After he finished breakfast, Billy joined the line of men who were carrying their plates and cups to the horse trough to rinse them out before returning them to Tom Miller, the heavy-set man who was furnishing the cutlery, carefully placing each cup and plate in his own pack behind his horse.

This was some army, Billy thought. It had no food, no uniforms, no guns, and no pay, and no horses, not even a saddle. Billy noticed that Poe Allen and Jim Allen both were having to ride bare-back because they didn't have saddles for their mounts.

Billy led Alexander back to the horse trough for a last drink, but Alexander took one look at the bits of bacon and eggs at the bottom of the horse trough and haughtily turned his head away from the trough that had been used to clean coffeecups and plates.

Billy started to mount Alexander; then he saw his mother, his father, little Andy, and Annette and Allison with their little pig-tailed heads staring around the side of their mother's hip. Billy led Alexander over close to the door. He started to mount again, but there was something in his mother's eye, a bit of moisture, that made him turn away from Alexander and walk to the door.

John King stuck his hand out toward Billy. "Take care of yourself, Son." John King shook Billy's hand.

Billy reached down and shook hands with four-year-old Andy King.

"You goin' away, Billy?" Andy tugged on Billy's britches leg.

"Yeah, I'll be gone for a little spell." Billy got down on his knees and placed both of his hands on his little brother's shoulders. "You take care of Ma, Pa, and your sisters while I'm gone. Hear me now?"

Andy King nodded his head.

Billy looked up at his two little sisters. "Allison, you and Annette will have to help Pa with the milking, and you'll have to help Ma with chopping the wood and gathering kindling. And you'll have to carry water from the well."

Allison and Annette nodded their blond pigtailed heads.

"You help Ma with the little one, now, you hear?"

Allison and Annette nodded their heads again.

Billy looked up at his mother, and he could see a tear streaming down one cheek. He rose to his feet slowly. He wiped his hands clean on the back of his britches, then put his arms around his mother. "Don't worry about me,

Ma." He patted his mother while she sobbed in his arms. "I'll put them Mexicans in their place and get home as quick as I can."

Billy felt little Andy tugging on his britches leg. He looked down.

"Will you bring me a Mexican saber?" Andy asked.

Billy looked at his mother, who suddenly stiffened and turned white at the word "saber."

"Yeah, Andy, I'll bring you a Mexican saber when I come home." Billy reached down and tusselled Andy's blonde hair. "Y'all be good now." Billy turned and mounted ole Alexander. He turned for a last look at his family, and he noticed that his mother was waving with one hand and shielding the tears in her eyes with the other hand.

Billy turned Alexander toward the gate and was about to kick him in the flanks to catch up with the volunteers who had already passed through the gate and turned northwest down the San Antonio Road.

As he turned at the gate, Billy stole one last look at his family. He saw his mother running toward the gate, holding both arms out.

Billy tossed her a wave, turned his horse at the gate, and was waving a last good-bye to his mother and father when he looked down and saw his dog, Comanche, wagging his long, shaggy tail.

"You can't go, Comanche. You'll have to stay here." Billy shook his finger at Comanche. "Now you go on back to the house."

Billy leaned over the saddle, staring at his dog. "Go home!" Billy shouted and waved his hand toward his family waiting near the front porch of the log cabin. "You'll have to stay here; you can't go with me," Billy scolded the dog.

Comanche just kept wagging his tail, waiting for Billy to race away so he could trot along beside him.

"Aw shucks!" Billy slid off of his horse. He led Alexander by the bridle reins back to the front porch. He stopped and looked at his pa. "Pa, you'll have to hold Comanche, or he'll go with me." Billy reached over and ruffled Comanche's black, wolf-like head.

"He'll be mighty hard to hold." Mr. King stepped off the porch and walked around Comanche, not touching him. He looked at Billy. "He's gonna try awful hard to go with you, wherever you go."

"Yeah, the trouble with Comanche is that he's no ordinary dog. He's an Indian dog. Leastways, he was an Indian dog. Now he's just my dog."

"I don't think he'll stay when you leave," Mrs. King ventured.

"He don't take kindly to nobody but me." Billy got down on his hands and knees and hugged the old dog's black head. "I healed his broken leg and pert near saved his life. I had to talk an awful long time just to talk him into eatin' food. He ain't very smart, but he sure is stubborn. He ain't taken up with nobody but me, has he, Ma?" Billy looked at his mother.

"No, Son, he's an Indian dog; he doesn't have but one master. You're the only master he has around here."

"Think you can hold him, Pa?" Billy rose to his feet and looked at his father. He noticed for the first time that he was nearly as tall as his father.

"I don't think anybody can hold him once you ride away." Mr. King spoke with misgiving eyes, leaning toward the dog, but not daring to touch him. "Maybe if we locked him in the house, he might stay 'til after you rode away."

Billy handed his bridle reins to his father. He led Comanche in the front door of the cabin. He shut the door suddenly and latched it on the outside. Billy raced down the front porch steps. He grabbed the bridle reins from his father, threw them over Alexander's head, vaulted in the saddle, and raced away. He waved his hand at his mother, father, little brother, and little sisters as he ducked under the oak limbs and rode through the gate, then headed west on the San Antonio road.

Just before he rounded a bend and disappeared out of view of the cabin, he glanced back and saw Comanche, his Indian dog, jump through the rawhide-covered east window of the cabin. The dog came racing and bounding toward Billy. Billy shook his head and smiled as he rode on down the San Antonio road.

Courtesy
Daughters of the
Republic of Texas Library,
San Antonio, Texas

CHAPTER IV

Billy kicked his heels into ole Alexander and got him up to a gallop until he rode beside Captain Kimball. Billy slowed Alexander down and saluted Captain Kimball. "Captain, Sir, can I stop and say good-bye to a friend of mine at the Anderson house?"

"You wanna stop at Frog-Eye Anderson's house?"

"Yes, Sir. I have a friend there I need to say good-bye to."

"Well, ole Frog-Eye ain't fit for military service."

"Yes, Sir, I know. He got kicked in the head by a mule. His head looks kinda like a broken egg shell."

"Well, we can't take him as a soldier."

"I don't want to talk to him as a soldier; I want to visit his daughter," Billy offered a bashful smile.

"Well, I was hoping we could just ride on by and pretend we just accidentally missed him." Captain Kimball rubbed his forehead with the palm of his hand, glad his forehead wasn't crushed like John Anderson's.

"Oh, but he ain't blind, Sir, really he ain't. He can see fifteen or twenty feet in front of him. Sometimes I think he can see further than that," Billy argued.

"Well, Private King, you can spend fifteen minutes there telling your girlfriend good-bye, but if ole Frog-Eye wants to know why we didn't stop and ask him to join us as an able-bodied man, you lie to him and tell him that you filled our quota, that we don't need any more men."

"Ole John'll ask."

"Well you're gonna have to start being a soldier awful early in life. You're gonna have to tell a lie your first day. You're gonna have to tell that man . . ."

"Captain Kimball, I'm just gonna tell him the truth. I'm just gonna tell him he can't see far enough and that you exempted him from service."

Captain Kimball shook his head. "You tell him that and he'll get on his horse and either shoot us or else make a liar out of both of us."

"I'll tell John that you said if you need him you'll send for him."

"Good boy." Captain Kimball slapped Billy on the back. "You give my respects to Mrs. Anderson and little Amy. And don't spent too long there courtin'." Captain Kimball waved him on his way.

Billy really gigged Alexander and told him to get down to that Anderson place in a hurry.

Billy left Alexander's reins tied at the gate of wooden stave posts and ran down the hill toward the Anderson house.

John Anderson was coming out of the barn with a milk bucket in his head. He held his head up high and turned slightly to the side to hear better. His brown hat was pulled down low, covering his forehead.

"That you, Billy?" John Anderson asked.

"Yes, Sir, Mr. Anderson. I've come by to say good-bye to Amy. I've joined the Texas Army."

"Oh?" John Anderson turned his head a little farther to the side in an effort to hear the number of horse hoofs and use his ears to count the number of men riding by his place. "I guess you want to talk to Amy." John Anderson forced a grin on the lower part of his face. His eyes were too ugly to smile. His forehead had been kicked and mashed in by a mule, and both of his eyes bugged out sort of like the raised eyes of a frog. They never smiled. "You'll find Amy in the barn milking cows."

Billy started racing toward the barn door, but John Anderson grabbed his arm as he went by. "Where's John King? Ain't he ridin' with you?"

"Naw, they ain't takin' old fuddy-duddies like you and

my pa. They're lettin' the young men fight this war."

"Oh?" John Anderson held on to Billy's arm. "You mean they don't need me?"

"No, Sir. Captain Kimball told me that if they needed you or my pa, they'd send for you."

"Well, I'll swan." John Anderson bent over low, studying the ground as he carried his bucket full of milk toward the house, so blind he was almost having to feel his way with his feet. "I wouldn't have thought they'd try to win a war without me."

Billy slipped into the barn quietly, trying to creep up on Amy, who was sitting on a three-legged wooden stool, milking the cow with her back to him. Billy was smiling as he crept silently across the straw-covered dirt floor, with his slender arms held up high. He crept up behind Amy and grinned as he looked down at her blonde pigtailed hair tied loosely with a leather thong.

Billy raised his hands high and tried to slip them over Amy's head to put them over her eyes so she couldn't see him.

The brown Swiss cow turned and stared at Billy, but Amy didn't move. He could hear her hands squeezing the rhythmical squirts of milk into the foamy bucket of milk. Billy placed his hands slowly and quietly over her eyes and squeezed tightly. He could feel her smile as he tighted his grip around her eyes.

"Guess who," Billy laughed.

Amy leaned back on her stool 'til her shoulders touched Billy's knees. She leaned her head back 'til her eyes peeked out under his hands. She smiled and blinked. "Billy King! What are you doing here this early in the morning?" She took the half-filled milk bucket from between her knees and set it on the ground safely away from the cow's hind legs. She rose slowly and turned her pretty freckled face toward Billy. "You got here too late to help with the milking." She reached for the milk bucket with one hand and reached for Billy's hand with the other.

"I've joined the Texas Army," Billy beamed proudly.

Amy set the milk bucket down and a frown of concern creased her face. "Oh no." She reached for both of Billy's hands.

"Yeah, I joined last night."

"But you're not old enough." Amy jerked on both of Billy's hands.

"Captain Kimball let me take my pa's place."

Amy shut both eyes and tightened her grip on Billy's hands. "When are you leaving?"

"I'm on my way right now."

"You going to the Alamo?"

Billy nodded.

Amy opened her eyes. "But I hear the whole Mexican army is there. There's thousands of 'em."

Billy nodded in agreement. "John Smith says it looked like the biggest herd of cows he ever saw."

"They're not cows." Amy picked up her milk bucket and led Billy out of the barn. She set the bucket down slowly and shut the barn door, dropping the wooden latch securely in place. "You're riding Alexander?" Amy inclined her head toward Billy's horse tied at the gate. "Comanche goin' to war too?" Amy pointed to Comanche waiting at the gate.

Billy nodded as he took the milk bucket from Amy and began carrying it for her. "Yeah, me and Comanche and ole Alexander are going to war."

Amy stopped and tugged on Billy's free hand. "But I won't let you go."

"But I done joined, Amy. I joined last night."

Billy set Amy's milk bucket down on the steps of the back porch.

"But what if you . . ."

"Aw shoot, Amy, them Mexicans don't know how to fight. Captain Kimball says we'll get there by daylight about March the first. We'll have 'em whupped and headed for home by the time the sun's two hands high."

"Come in and take breakfast with us. Let's talk about this." Amy picked up the milk bucket and opened the back door of the Anderson cabin.

"No thanks, Amy. I've done had breakfast. I just came by to . . . to . . ."

Amy blushed. The freckles darkened on her light-skinned, pretty face. "You came by to kiss me good-bye." Amy folded her arms across her chest.

Billy nodded. He shrugged his shoulders and grinned sheepishly at Amy. "That an' I just came by to tell you I was leaving."

"Well, I ain't kissin' no soldiers." Amy tightened her folded arms across her chest.

"Well, in that case, I just wanted to tell you good-bye. I'll be gone a spell."

"You may not come back."

Billy turned his head to the side with a shrug of acceptance. "I guess I just wanted to say good-bye."

"Can't you come in for a glass of milk or a cup of coffee?"

Billy shook his head. "Captain Kimball's done rode off and left me. I've gotta hurry and catch up." Billy stepped down off the back porch.

Amy lowered her arms from her defiant stance. Her hands rose slowly toward Billy's retreating figure.

"Billy! Wait!" She ran to Billy, grabbing him with both arms. She turned him slowly and shut her eyes. A tear streamed down her cheek as she kissed Billy beside his ear.

Billy turned and took her face in both his hands and kissed her on the lips.

"I'm awful, aren't I?" Amy blushed and smiled.

Amy had both arms around Billy, clinging to him as tears ran down her cheeks and dropped slowly on her white blouse.

Billy reached over and wiped the wet spot off the bottom of her chin.

"I couldn't go. I just couldn't go without..."

Amy nodded.

"I'm glad you came by." Amy blinked a tearful smile. "I'm even glad I kissed you."

"I'm glad you did, too," Billy grinned.

"Can I give you a gift, something to remember me by, a garter, a ribbon, a scarf, so that even if I don't see you, if you don't come back, a bit of me will be with you? Always?"

"What for?" Billy asked.

"So you'll have it to hold onto. Maybe it'll bring you good luck."

Billy reached up and untied the yellow ribbon from Amy's soft hair. He tied it around his neck slowly.

Billy leaned forward and gave Amy a quick kiss on the lips, then turned and ran toward Alexander, waving at Comanche, who was sitting on his haunches at the wooden gate. Even Alexander was nodding his head in farewell. "Tell your ma and pa I'll stop by on my way home from the war."

Amy walked around the house, walking slowly toward the gate, but Billy climbed through the gate and got on Alexander and rode away without ever once looking back.

Amy wondered if his eyes were as wet as hers. She turned and went into the house.

CHAPTER V

Billy was riding behind Captain Kimball, admiring his white horse, his rifle, and his two silver-handled pistols. Billy wondered how come a hat-maker from New York City had become so wealthy and so influential in the town of Gonzales that he could afford the fastest horse and the finest guns. Billy wondered, so he asked Galba Fuqua.

"How come Kimball is a Captain, when all he knows how to do is make hats?"

"Captain Kimball makes a very good hat, a strong and dependable hat. It don't shrink in the rain, it don't blow off in the wind, if it get gets dirty, you just wipe it clean, it can be used to carry water, and it'll last ten or fifteen years."

"But Galba, you didn't answer my question. I know he's a good hat-maker; I'm wearing one of his black hats myself." Billy reached up and felt of his father's big black hat. "But why is he a Captain? Why is he in command of this bunch of soldiers?"

"Well, I don't know about that. All I know is that he got elected." Galba Fuqua stuck his chin up in the air. "Everybody knows that whatever Captain Kimball does, he does it well. We figured if he started out to take us to the Alamo, he'd get us there."

"But if something happens to Captain Kimball, who's gonna make hats?" Billy reached up and felt of his father's big, black hat. He and Galba smiled at each other.

John Smith rode up beside Captain Kimball and waved him a salute. "Captain, we gonna stop at Michael Lomis' place? He's got a big family, lots of fine strong boys. His place is just this side of the Guadalupe River."

"He's Catholic, isn't he?"

"Yeah, Irish Catholic."

"Well, I don't care what his religion is. It's my job to stop by his place and ask for all able-bodied volunteers. I can't ride to the relief of the Alamo without stopping at every farm along the way and giving every able-bodied man an opportunity to ride with me."

"Yes, Sir."

Captain Kimball turned his white palomino horse toward the Loomis place, and as he did so, Billy kicked his heels into Alexander.

"Sir, can I ride down to the Loomis place with you?"

Captain Kimball jerked up on his reins, causing his palomino to rear. "Naw, I don't think anybody had better accompany me. There might be a shootin' down there."

"But Captain Kimball, I know Pat Loomis real well."

Captain Kimball studied the road leading down to the Guadalupe River bottom. The crack of a heavy axe chopping wood boomed from the river valley.

"Well, you might as well come on. Maybe both of us will get shot." Captain Kimball waved for Billy to follow him down to the Michael Loomis place on the south side of the Guadalupe River.

"Pat Loomis wants to go. I just know he wants to go." Billy spoke to Captain Kimball as they kicked their horses into a fast gallop.

The Loomis place was a long three-room log cabin with huge doors, but with just holes where windows were supposed to be. The windows were not glass, but deer hide hung over the openings to protect them from the cold, and yet let in a little light. Water was piped to the house in a hollowed-out half log from the spring. Water trickled from a cliffside spring and ran downhill in the hollowed-out log to the kitchen window.

Two chickens were perched on the log waterway, leading into the house, dipping their heads, drinking water.

There were chickens and hogs everywhere, all over the place, and several goats. Billy smiled as he watched six-year-old Andy Loomis riding a white goat, holding on to the goat's horns with one small hand.

"Get off and come in." Michael Loomis rose from a hide-covered chair on the front porch and held up his hand as Captain Kimball brought his horse to a halt at the hitching rack.

"No, really we don't have time." Captain Kimball cut his eyes toward the two tall Loomis twins, Pat and Mike, who were chopping wood at the wood rack just east of the back porch. Captain Kimball raised his voice as he spoke. "We're on our way from Gonzales to relieve the garrison at the Alamo. I just stopped by to see if you had any able-bodied men that would like to volunteer."

The wood-chopping stopped at once. Pat and Mike Loomis shouldered their axes and walked around the south side of the house.

Grey-haired Michael Loomis, Sr. shook his head. "No, we have no able-bodied men who would like to fight the Catholic army of Santa Anna." Michael Loomis, Sr. moved around between his twin sons and Captain Kimball.

"But Pa, I'd like to go." Pat Loomis set his axe on his shoulder and tried to walk around his father, but wherever Pat moved, his father stepped in front of him.

"Mr. Kimball, there are four able-bodied men here—myself and my three sons—but I would shoot them right between the eyes before I'd let them go fight fellow-Catholics."

"But Pa, I wanna go." Pat pushed his way around his father. "There's Billy King; he's going."

"You can't go, Son. Now you get back to chopping wood."

Pat Loomis eyed his father defiantly. "If Billy King's old enough to go, I'm old enough to go, too."

"You ain't goin', Pat, not to this stupid, useless, unnecessary war. It's a hopeless cause."

"But Pa."

"Mike, go bring me my gun." Michael Loomis, Sr. pointed his finger at the open front door. Then he turned toward Captain Kimball as Mike walked slowly and unhappily toward the door. "Mr. Kimball, if you ain't gone when that gun gets out here, I'll put a hole in your head for trying to break up my family."

Captain Kimball folded his arms across his chest, as he studied Michael Loomis, then he grasped his saddlehorn. "Do you realize, Sir, that failure to volunteer when all able-bodied men are asked to volunteer can result in the loss of your land grant?"

Michael Loomis laughed. "This Irishman ain't got no land grant. All I've got is a strong back and a thick head. If anybody ever comes and tries to take his land I've hacked out of this river bottom," he waved his hand at the cleared bottomland, "if anybody comes down here and tries to take my land, they'll find a rifle pointing around the trunk of every tree." He planted his feet wide apart and tightened his jaws. "You Protestants would find you got an honest war on your hands. An Irish war!"

Captain Kimball raised his bridle reins. He nodded toward Michael Loomis, Sr. "Thank you, Mr. Loomis, for your time and your courtesy. We'll be ridin' on." He turned and rode back toward the highway.

Billy waved at Pat Loomis. "Pat, I'll bring you a Mexican saber when I come home." Billy kicked Alexander and rode toward the highway as fast as Alexander would take him.

CHAPTER VI

When they reached the ford of the Guadalupe River, Captain Kimball held up one arm. He surveyed the swirling, deep river with its white chalky banks. He turned and studied his men, now dismounting and leading their horses to the water. The men got on their hands and knees beside their horses and drank from the cool, spring-fed river.

"Is there anybody here who can't swim?" Captain Kimball held up both hands for attention. "The Guadalupe's up. It'll be over our horses' backs out there in the middle. We're gonna have to do a little swimmin' to reach the other bank."

The men glanced around at each other.

Galba Fuqua walked forward with his head down. He stood beside the river, staring at the deep, blue, fast-moving water. After a long study, he raised his arm. A murmnur of laughs broke the stillness.

"You can't swim son?" Captain Kimball walked over and put his arm on Galba's shoulder.

Galba Fuqua shook his head without raising it. Finally he raised his head and looked at Captain Kimball. "I never did learn to swim. I never did have no chance. I was raised in a horse stable, and I didn't have no daddy to teach me like Billy here had." He pointed at his friend, Billy King. He was trying not to show his hurt and embarrassment.

"Well, I don't think you'd better try to cross if you can't swim. That water's six or eight foot deep out there in the middle, and it's movin' mighty fast." Captain Kimball kept his hand on Galba's shoulder.

"I just never did learn how." Galba's face puckered up and a tear ran down his cheek.

Captain Kimball turned to John Smith. "What're we gonna do about these boys that can't swim?"

John Smith shook his head. "There's no need in him getting out there in that deep, swift-running water if he can't swim."

Billy gathered Alexander's reins and led him between Galba Fuqua and Captain Kimball. "Captain, Sir, I swim real good, and so does ole Alexander. If somebody else would lead Galba's horse across, an' carry his gun, Galba could hold on to one side of Alexander while I hold on to the other side. Ole Alexander could swim plum across the ocean." Billy smiled and put his arm around Galba Fuqua's waist.

"Well, what'd'ya say, Son? Do you wanna turn back or do you wanna try to cross that river?" Kimball asked.

Galba Fuqua shook his head. "I don't know, Sir. I ain't afraid of no Mexicans, but that river's something else." Galba reached up with his shirt sleeve and wiped a tear off his cheek.

"If you have to turn back, Galba," Billy asked excitedly, "can I have your gun?"

"'Taint mine. Captain Kimball lent it to me in Gonzales; you'll have to ask him."

"Captain Kimball," Billy placed his hand on Galba's gun and turned to the hat-maker, "if Galba can't swim an' can't cross the river an' he has to turn back, can I have his gun? He says you only lent it to him."

Billy had a grip on the gun stock, but Galba jerked it away.

"Maybe I can't swim," Galba pulled the gun to his chest, "but I ain't afraid to fight. If somebody'd just get me acrost that river, I wouldn't be afraid of nothing no more."

Billy's hand was still held up high, reaching where the gun had been. He lowered his hand slowly. He saw Galba clutching the long rifle to his chest. "You want me to help you across the river?"

Galba nodded.

Billy sighed, nodding his head. "I guess the Lord intended me to be a cannon boy instead of a rifleman.

Billy led Alexander between himself and Galba. "Galba, I tell you what you do. You hand your gun to Captain Kimball an' you hold on to the saddlehorn on that side of ole Alexander and I'll hold on to this side. We'll wade out there in the water, and when it gets too deep to walk, you just hang on to that saddlehorn and keep your head out of the water. Me and Alexander'll take you across."

Galba Fuqua looked at Billy with blue Jewish eyes that seemed to smile. A grin of thanks and appreciation creased the corners of his mouth. He nodded as he handed his rifle to Captain Kimball. "Would you carry my rifle across?" Kimball nodded and cradled Galba's rifle in his arm.

Billy waded Alexander out into the water. He waved his free hand for Galba to follow. When they were waist-deep in the water, Billy turned to Galba. "Now you just hold on with both hands, and don't do nothin' but hang on. Me and Alexander'll take you across.

"We goin' first?" Galba turned and stared at the men waiting on the south side of the river.

"Yeah, let's show 'em how to cross the Guadalupe."

Galba shut both eyes and grabbed the leather-covered saddle-horn with both hands.

"It's cold, ain't it?" Billy yelled as the water deepened to their shoulders.

Alexander stepped off into a deep hole and his rump disappeared under the water. He raised his head high and began swimming and drifting slowly downstream.

"Come on, Alexander, come on boy," Billy shouted above the splashing water. "Swim hard, boy. We've got an extra passenger."

Galba Fuqua was trying to climb onto Alexander's shoulders. He kicked his feet and held the saddlehorn with one hand and Alexander's mane with the other hand, trying to keep himself out of the cold, rolling water.

Billy shifted the bridle reins and turned Alexander's head more upstream than directly across the river. Billy could feel Alexander's sides heave as he churned the water. The horse seemed to understand as he hit the swift centerstream of the river, paddling his feet rapidly.

They hit a deep swirl, and Alexander's body disappeared. Only his head and the top part of his neck stayed above the swift-moving stream.

Galba's head disappeared under the water for an instant. When he came up with his eyes shut and spitting water, he began climbing Alexander's neck.

"No!" Billy screamed. He grabbed at Galba's hand and pulled it free of Alexander's neck. Galba had such a tight grip, he nearly pulled Alexander's head under the water before Billy jerked the hand loose and put it back on the saddlehorn.

Billy took his hand off the saddlehorn so Galba could have a good grip. "Just keep your head above water, just keep your head up. We're more'n half way across," Billy spat water as he shouted and patted Galba's tight grip on the saddlehorn.

They were now thirty yards downstream, drifting in the current. Alexander's head and shoulders reared suddenly as he found footing on the north bank. The sudden clamber of Alexander caught Galba unaware. His hand slipped off the saddlehorn. Galba shut his eyes and thrashed the water.

Billy leaned across the saddle and grabbed one of Galba's arms. He pulled him toward the saddle. Alexander started climbing out of the water with Billy leaning across the saddle holding Galba's arm and dragging him out of the water onto the north shore. Alexander stomped his feet and began shaking his body, shaking the water off.

Galba Fuqua opened his eyes and stared at the ground. "We made it! We made it!" Galba shouted.

"Twasn't nothin' to it, was it?" Billy grinned across the saddle at Galba.

Galba looked at Billy as they pushed away from Alexander. "I lost my grip."

"Yeah, I forgot to tell you that when a horse starts climbing out on the other side, he really jerks hard. You just wasn't ready for it. I should of told you."

Galba nodded as other horsemen began climbing out of the water.

"Didn't have no trouble at all, did you boy?" Captain Kimball pounded Billy on the back.

"Nope, didn't have no trouble at all." Billy agreed and cast a sly knowing glance at Galba Fuqua.

"Alright now," Captain Kimball turned in his saddle and looked at the men who had just climbed on shore. "We'll have to build a fire, dry our powder and our clothes, and get our guns oiled. We'll take a two-hour break and rest our horses. Somebody go get a turkey or deer for pot-lickin'."

Courtesy
Daughters of the
Republic of Texas Library,
San Antonio, Texas

CHAPTER VII

"Captain, Sir, there's riders ahead." Jimmy Allen was racing his horse back down the line, kicking his mount for faster speed, grasping the horse's mane with one hand, flipping the bridle reins with the other hand. He pulled up on his reins and brought his horse to a rearing stop in front of Captain Kimball, waving his arms and shouting. "They's riders ahead; I seen 'em myself," Jim Allen shouted and pointed up the road he had just raced down.

"Riders?" Captain Kimball raised his hand for a stop and put his other hand over his ear for better hearing. "Are they coming toward us, or are they going the same way we're going?"

"I don't know, Sir," Jim Allen answered.

"What'd ya mean you don't know? Were they Mexican troops? Were they in uniform? Were they coming toward us?" the Captain shouted.

"I don't know," Jim Allen answered with a shrug of his arm. "I just seen 'em and turned and bolted back down this way to tell you they was there."

"Settle down now, Son; I need to know what you saw. They may be Mexican troops, and if they were Mexican troops, I gotta know it." Captain Kimball pointed his gloved hand at Jim Allen.

"Were they in uniform? Did you see any green and white uniforms?"

Captain Kimball rose high in his stirrups, trying to see over the hill, trying to make out what manner of men were waiting down the road. He slumped back into his saddle, staring at the ground for an instant. Then he looked at Jim Allen. "You saw their clothes?"

"Yes, Sir."

"Was they wearing home-spuns and buckskins?"

"Don't know. Don't know whether I saw—home-spuns and buckskins or not. I jest saw men ahead."

"Home-spuns an' buckskins sounds like our side, but I think we'd better go forward and take a look." Captain Kimball turned his gaze toward John Smith. "Jim Allen and I are going to ride forward and see what's waitin' for us on the other side of that hill. If you don't hear no shots, y'all just come ridin' on. But if you hear shots, you better scatter. It'll be Mexican cavalrymen."

John Smith nodded his head and tossed a salute at Captain Kimball. He waved his arm away from the road. "Everybody get off the road. Get behind a tree and get your gun ready. If that's Mexican cavalry, it means they've done took the Alamo and they're comin' after us. Everybody get behind a tree and get your gun cocked and loaded."

Billy King held both hands out toward John Smith. "But Sir, I ain't got a gun."

"Well, get behind that tree and wish you had a gun," John Smith ordered, pointing his gloved hand at a big, red, oak tree.

Billy and Galba Fuqua ended up together behind the red oak tree. Galba was holding his gun by the barrel, trying to charge it with gunpowder. His horse was prancing and dancing and wouldn't hold still. Galba was missing the barrel with the gunpowder.

"I can't load no gun on no horse," Galba fumed.

Billy laughed as he watched Galba nervously miss the gun barrel with his powder horn. He held out his hand toward Galba. "Here, let me have it. I'll load it for you." Billy climbed off of Alexander and held the rifle between his legs as he charged the gun with two dips of gunpowder. Then he pulled the ramrod out, placed a cloth over the tip of it, and pushed it down into the gun barrel. He rammed it solidly against the gunpowder. Then he lifted a ball out of Galba's ball bag. He rolled it down the gun barrel, then put a cloth over the tip of the ramrod again. He pushed the ramrod down and rammed the ball firmly against the gunpowder. Billy lifted the rifle, feeling of its weight. "Seems powerful strange to be going to war and having no gun." He charged the powder hole and handed the rifle to Galba.

Galba reached for the gun with trembling fingers and almost dropped it.

Billy and Galba watched Jim Allen and Captain Kimball ride slowly down the road and disappear over the hill. After they had disappeared, Billy glanced around at the men crouched behind trees. None of them were well-hidden.

"I'm gonna have something to fight with." Billy looked up into the oak tree and spied a dead limb. He kicked Alexander and rode him over to where the broken limb hung down. He grabbed the limb, then rose in the saddle and jerked and kicked until he broke the limb off. He brushed away the little branches, then hefted the broken limb by the small end like a sledge hammer. "It ain't exactly a sword, but it's better'n nothin'." He wondered how he would guide Alexander and still be able to swing his club with both hands, if a troop of Mexican cavalry should suddenly come charging over the hill, waving their swords and pistols and rifles.

At that instant, he saw Jim Allen riding over the hill toward them in a slow, calm lope waving his arms. "Come on!" he shouted, stopping his horse and waving for the men to follow him on down the road. "Come on. It weren't no Mexicans. It was just three men from Liberty and three men from San Felipe. They were just settin' at the side of the road eatin' pecans, restin' their horses and waitin' for us to come along."

"No Mexicans?" Galba Fuqua lowered his trembling

rifle. He kicked his horse and rode out from behind the red oak tree. "I don't believe you was scared, Billy." Galba glanced at Billy King.

"Naw, I wasn't scared. I was just mad. I was just mad 'cause I didn't have no gun."

"Was you gonna fight them with that club?" Galba nodded toward the oak club Billy still had lying across Alexander' neck.

"That was all I could find," Billy laughed.

They topped the hill and rode down the road toward a huge pecan tree beside the road where six men were still sitting in the shade cracking pecans between two rocks and talking to Captain Kimball.

Galba moved close to Billy and cupped his hand around his mouth so nobody could hear what he said except Billy. "Billy, what would you have done if a Mexican cavalryman had made a razoo at you with a saber?" Galba looked at Billy with wide, scared eyes.

"Aw, I don't know." Billy smiled as he looked down at his long oak club. "Well, if a Mexican cavalryman had taken after me, I would have swung this club and tried to get to him before he got to me with that saber. I'd have tried to knock him off his horse, at least knock him away from that saber. Then I'd try to pick it up and run it through him."

Galba looked at Billy for a long, thoughtful instant. "You would've done it, wouldn't you?"

"I don't know whether I would have done it or not. I just know I'd have tried to do it."

"Yeah, I believe you would've." Galba looked at his trembling hand and wondered what he would have done.

Billy and Galba were riding beside John Smith when they reached the pecan tree where all the men had gathered.

Captain Kimball rode his horse toward John Smith. "Well, we've added six more men to our relief column."

Captain Kimball beamed at John Smith. "The three Taylor brothers are from Liberty." Captain Kimball pointed at the three youngest men sitting on their knees cracking pecans and eating them like they were famished.

"Where are those other three from?" John Smith asked.

Captain Kimball pointed at the man in grey homespun. "Well, one of 'em's name is William Summers. He says the jailer let him out of jail down at San Felipe so he could go to the relief of the Alamo garrison."

"And the other two?" John Smith asked.

"Well, they were in jail with Summers. They were all three let out to go to the relief of the Alamo."

"Is three men all we've got from San Felipe, and just three from Liberty?" John Smith looked askance at the six men who were still breaking pecans. "That's not much of a relief force, is it?"

"Well, it's six more men." Captain Kimball looked north-westward down the San Antonio road. "This is just the first group of men we've come across. We'll run on to other men on down the road. There'll be lots of other men."

"I hope so." John Smith shifted unhappily in his saddle. "We're gettin' powerfully close to San Antonio, and we ain't got but thirty-two men. Our thirty-two-man relief contingent will raise the Alamo garrison to the grand sum of a hundred and eighty-two men. That ain't gonna make much of a dent in a Mexican army of three or four thousand." He glared unhappily at the six men still eating pecans under the pecan tree. "I'd have thought we'd got fifty men from San Felipe, and at least thirty from Liberty."

"Aw well, John, the only real hope we've got is that Fannin's moved his five hundred men from Goliad to the Alamo. If he hasn't got there with those five hundred men, our little army of men an' boys ain't gonna make no difference."

Billy and Galba had their pockets full of pecans when Captain Kimball turned his horse northwestward and resumed the march toward San Antonio.

"Were you really let out of jail?" Galba Fuqua asked the man Captain Kimball had pointed out as William Summers.

"Yeah, Sheriff John Longstreet figured I was gonna hang for killin' a cotton broker, and he just figured it'd be a little cheaper on the county if instead of hanging me, he just turned me loose to get killed at the Alamo."

"You killed a man?" Galba asked.

Gruff, bearded William Summers nodded his head. "Shore did, son. This here cotton broker offered me five cents a pound for my cotton. I thought that was about half of what it was really worth, and I just picked up the chair I was settin' in and hit him over the head with it. I didn't know it was an oak chair. Broke his neck."

"You mean it killed him?"

"Naw," William Summers spoke through his heavy black beard, "they just buried him alive so they'd have some reason to hang me."

"Buried him alive!" Galba Fuqua gasped.

"Yep, buried him alive so they could hang me."

"Did they really?" Billy asked.

William Summers shook his head. "Naw, the minute that oak chair didn't shatter, I knew I'd done killed me a cotton broker." He wrinkled his forehead and took a second look at Billy King.

"I ain't got a gun." Billy volunteered, looking at the rifle in Summers' hand.

"No gun?" William Summers shook his head, then laughed. "Son, you better go kill a man like I did, then talk the sheriff into lettin' you go to the relief of the Alamo, and maybe he'll give you a gun like I got one."

"You mean the sheriff let you out of jail, then gave you a gun?" Billy asked.

William Summers nodded his head and raised his long-barrelled rifle.

Billy and Alexander stomped at the flies at the same time.

Courtesy Daughters of the Republic of Texas Library, San Antonio, Texas

CHAPTER VIII

"We're getting close to San Antonio, Son. What're we gonna do about that dog?" Captain Kimball pointed at Billy's dog, Comanche.

"What about my dog?" Billy looked at Comanche and then at Captain Kimball.

Captain Kimball shook his head. "You can't take that dog in the Alamo. We'd never get through the Mexican lines. He'd start barking at Mexican dogs, or Mexican soldiers, or Mexican horses. And the first bark he makes will give us away."

"Comanche won't bark." Billy stopped Alexander and climbed off quickly. He gathered Comanche in both arms, then walked back to his horse clutching his dog against his chest. "He won't bark if I tell him not to." Billy tossed Comanche across Alexander's neck and vaulted into the saddle. He grabbed his dog and pulled him against him. "I'll hold him here in the saddle where I can squeeze him so tight he can't bark, and if he tries to bark, I'll put my hand over his muzzle."

"You gonna risk the lives of thirty-two men just to carry a dog into the Alamo?" Captain Kimball asked.

Billy shook his head, feeling several eyes studying him and his dog.

"We may even have to leave the horses behind." Captain Kimball patted his horse and looked at John W. Smith. "What'd'ya think, Smitty? Will we be able to get through with our horses?"

"It depends on the moon. If there's a bright moon, we may not be able to get in there with or without horses." John Smith pushed back his black hat and turned his head from side to side as he studied the low dark clouds. "If it stays dark and cloudy, we might be able to get in with our horses. We might even be able to get in with that boy's dog."

Billy nuzzled his chin down against Comanche's ears and smiled at John Smith.

"Can't take any chances on a barking dog." Kimball shook his head.

"Comanche and I've been together a long time." Billy felt his chin begin to tremble, and his eyes filled with tears. He sniffed. "He's been my dog for more'n two years. He's an Indian dog; he don't take up with nobody but me. He was with the Comanches when they raided the Sutton place two years ago this coming March 2nd. He got shot or something hit him; when we found him he had a broken leg. I rode with Pa when we trailed the Comanches. We followed 'em for more'n ten miles, but we never caught no Comanches. All we caught was this Comanche." Billy squeezed his dog and nuzzled his chin against his ears. "Comanche was hoppin' around on three legs. Mr. Sutton wanted to shoot him, said he was going to die anyway. I asked Pa if I could catch him. He just laughed and said, 'Yeah, if you can catch him, you can have him.' I didn't try to catch him; I just talked him into coming to me. I carried him home and splintered his leg. I slept on the front porch with him. He'd drink water, but he wouldn't eat. Never ate nothin' for a week. Then one Sunday afternoon I offered him a chicken bone and he ate it, and he's been my dog ever since." Billy leaned back and looked at his dog. "He looks like a wolf, but he ain't really a wolf." Billy grinned at him. "He's just an Indian dog named Comanche."

"Bein' as he's an Indian dog, shootin' him won't make much difference. You gonna shoot him, or you want me to shoot him?" Captain Kimball asked Billy.

Billy stopped his horse and stared at Captain Kimball. "I don't want him shot." Billy's chin began to tremble again. "He ain't no Indian dog; he's my dog."

"You ain't gonna be able to get through them Mexican lines with no barking dog."

"If you don't mind, Sir, me and Alexander and Comanche will be the last ones to go in. We'll stay 'way back, Sir, and we won't bark or move or say anything until everybody else gets in the Alamo."

"We need to take our horses in," John Smith surveyed the line of men and horses, "so we can carry in all our ammunition. And besides, we don't wanna leave no horses outside for them Mexican cavalrymen." John W. Smith grinned his big black-toothed grin. "I think if we can take the horses in, surely we can take one dog."

"Alright then, Smitty, you'll be responsible for that dog," Captain Kimball warned.

John W. Smith nodded. "I don't think any man oughta have to go where he can't take his dog. And besides, there's a little road leadin' into that north portal. Jim Bonham has travelled it so often we call it the Jim Bonham road. 'Course, it ain't really a road; it's just a deep, narrow canyon. But fortunately it runs close to that north portal. And as long as ole Davy Crockett's standin' up there sharp-shooting from that north wall, they ain't gonna be no Mexicans on that side of the fort. Leastwise, not no live Mexicans. Santa Anna's men hauled away about a dozen men's carcasses 'fore they found out Crockett was guardin' that north wall. Them Mexicans learned to keep a respectful distance from where Crockett and his Tennessee Mounted Volunteers was standin' guard. They stay back about half a mile and flinch and duck ever' time a shot is fired."

"You mean there's a canyon that leads into the Alamo?" Captain Kimball asked.

"Well, no; it don't rightly lead right into the Alamo. But it leads real close to that north portal of the Alamo. And as long as Crockett is standin' guard up there on top of that wall, them Mexicans stay out of that canyon."

"How do we get there?" Captain Kimball asked.

"Well, when we get to Powder House Hill about a mile from the Alamo, we turn north. I'll give a coyote howl to let the boys inside the Alamo know we're out here. They'll get a little commotion goin' so nobody'll hear us. Then in the racket we'll take off down that canyon and maybe be able to ride into the Alamo without even bein' shot at."

"You mean you've got a signal between you and the Alamo?"

"Naw, I've just got a signal between me and Davy Crockett," Smitty replied. "We're not very good coyote howlers. I know his coyote howl and he knows my coyote howl."

"You make gettin' in sound easy," Captain Kimball commented.

"Well, gettin' in's a lot easier than gettin' out." Smitty shifted his reins and turned his horse toward Powder House Hill.

Courtesy
Daughters of the
Republic of Texas Library,
San Antonio, Texas

CHAPTER IX

"Whew! Look at all the campfires!" Billy King gasped as he pointed his hand at the long rows of campfires, lighting the night sky.

"Wow! Look at the tents!" Jimmy Allen lowered his reins and let his horse graze the lush grass on the western side of Powder House Hill.

The white tents were set well back in neat orderly rows well away from the campfires lining the west bank of the silvery San Antonio River.

"Well, Smitty, what'd'ya think?" Captain Kimball pulled his horse up and looked at John W. Smith. "Are there more here now than there were when you left?"

"Can't tell in the dark," Smitty answered.

A cannon belched its yellow arc of flame from its revetment on the west side of the San Antonio River, causing the horses to jerk and rear.

"Well, that cannon mean's they ain't taken the Alamo," John W. Smith patted his horse's neck.

"It looks awful dark in there." Captain Kimball raised his hand to shield his eyes from the campfires to better study the white-walled Alamo. "You sure the garrison's still inside that old fort?"

"Yeah, they're still there," Smitty replied. "Colonel Travis don't believe in lightin' the place up. He likes to keep them walls dark so them Mexicans can't see his marksmen. Them boys from Kentucky and Tennessee can shoot just as good in the dark as they can in the daylight. 'Specially Crockett's boys from Tennessee. That's why we're gonna have to head around to the east and come in toward that north wall."

"We gonna have any trouble takin' our horses in?" Billy held on to Comanche with one arm and patted Alexander with the other hand.

"Can't tell yet, Son," Smitty replied. "I won't know 'til we work our way around to the northeast corner of the Alamo. Then I'll give a couple o' coyote howls. And then I'll have to set there and wait and see how many howls Crockett throws back at me. If he just gives one howl, that means wait. If he gives two howls, that means come on in. And if he gives three coyote howls, that means don't come in." Smitty looked at Captain Kimball.

"What does three coyote howls mean?" Captain Kimball asked.

"Well, Sir," Smitty shifted in his saddle, grasping the saddlehorn with both hands, "three coyote howls means there ain't no comin' in, for us not to try."

"What do we do if there's three coyote howls?" Galba Fuqua asked.

"Well, if Crockett gives three coyote howls, that means the only road going into the Alamo has been closed by the Mexicans. They ain't but one way to get in, and that's on that low road down through that canyon that leads close to the north portal. If it's been closed by the Mexicans, there ain't no gettin' into the Alamo."

"What do we do if we get three coyote howls?" Captain Kimball asked.

John W. Smith slumped in his saddle and stared at his hands folded on his saddlehorn. "I reckon three coyote howls means we'd better go home."

"You mean just go off and leave Crockett, Bowie, Travis and their men locked up in there?" Captain Kimball asked.

"Well they'll be the ones tellin' us not to try to get in. That's all I know," Smitty replied.

Smitty led the party back into the woods as they circled far to the east, and then headed north. He stopped in the clearing and watched the fires and torches surrounding the white-walled Alamo. He climbed off his horse and whispered. "The woods are gettin' thicker and thicker. I think we'd better dismount and lead our horses, or these limbs will pull us out of our saddles."

Billy grasped Comanche with both hands. He looked at Jim Allen and whispered, "What am I gonna do with Comanche if I have to get off and walk? I can't carry him and hold my horse."

"You better not set him down on the ground, because if he starts barkin', we've had it." Jim Allen climbed off his horse. He cradled his rifle in his right arm and led his horse with his left hand.

Billy slid off of Alexander and grunted, "Oh, he's too heavy to carry." Billy clung to Comanche with both hands as the dog wiggled and tried to jump to the ground. Billy clung to the kicking, scratching Comanche. He had to press down with his head and chin to hold the dog secure.

Comanche began to whimper. He was tired of being carried. He wanted to get on the ground where he could run.

"I know what I'll do." Billy climbed off and set Comanche on the ground and straddled him with both legs. He took the end of one long bridle rein and tied it around Comanche's neck, securing it with a fast knot. "There now, you can run on the ground, and yet you can't go anywhere. You'll have to stay with me and Alexander," Billy spoke to his dog.

Comanche ran to the end of the bridle rein, and he whimpered when the rein tightened and jerked him backward.

"You shut up." Billy put a finger to his lips. "If you say another word, I'm gonna tell Alexander to bite you right between the ears."

Comanche's long black ears stiffened and flipped lightly. He looked at Alexander, then lowered his head and began to pant with his red tongue hanging out as he trotted along beside Billy.

Billy was now guiding both his horse and his dog through the pine-covered hills a mile east of the Alamo.

"How much farther is it?" young Edward Taylor complained as he recovered his hat after running into a moss-covered oak limb that jutted out over the path.

"I don't know," Jim Allen replied, leading his horse beside Edward Taylor.

"Well, I'm tired. I'm tired and hungry and sleepy and thirsty," growled Edward Taylor. He was the youngest of the three Taylor brothers from Liberty. "I ain't had nothin' to eat but a handful of pecans since I left home."

"It's bound to be midnight." Jim Allen shielded his eyes as he stared up at the dark, cloud-covered sky. "We've rode more than two miles since it got dark."

"This is the last time I'm goin' to war." Edward Taylor jerked on his bridle reins, hurrying his horse through the tangled underbrush.

"You'd better hope it's not your last time to go to war," Galba Fuqua volunteered.

Looking ahead in the dark night, Billy could see that the horses were beginning to form a circle around Smitty.

"There still ain't any Mexican cannons located around here on the north side." John W. Smith noted with satisfaction, "I 'spect ole Davy Crockett kept pickin' off them cannoneers 'til they decided this wasn't a good place to locate a cannon." Smitty took off his hat and rubbed his forehead on his shirt sleeve. "It's three-quarters of a mile of hard fast ridin' to that door at the east end of that north wall. Can you see it?" Smitty pointed his hat at the dark door at the eastern end of the north wall.

Some of the men shifted their horses for a better look at the small door on the north wall.

"It don't look big enough to let a horse through," Jim Allen volunteered.

"It'll get bigger as you get closer to it," Smitty informed him.

"I want to say a few words." Captain Kimball held up one arm for attention. "You're all volunteers." Captain Kimball spoke quietly and held both hands up as if he was about to close his eyes and pray. "Every man among you volunteered to come to the relief of the Alamo garrison." Captain Kimball stopped and gazed for a moment at fifteen-year-old Billy King. "I'm proud to call you men." He nodded his head at Billy. "Bein' as you are volunteers, I have to ask you one more time before I lead you into the Alamo. Is there any man among you who wishes to turn back? If there is such a man, all you have to do is hold up your hand, turn your horse to the south, and ride away."

Billy noticed William Summers, the man from the San Felipe jail, cut his eyes at the woods to the south. Summers licked his lips, then spoke. "I've got a lotta kids, and a wife that's expectin'."

Captain Kimball shook his head. "Summers, you're one man that ain't a volunteer. The only reason you're here is because they didn't wanna have to stretch a rope down at San Felipe. You don't have a right to leave."

"I got an expectant wife and a lotta little kids," William Summers argued.

"Well, what'd'ya think?" Captain Kimball turned and looked at John W. Smith.

"I don't want Summers or anybody else ridin' in with me unless he wants to." John Smith spat.

William Summers rubbed his bearded chin. "I guess I'd rather ride in there than go back to San Felipe and look at that rope."

"Is there anybody else here who's got some reason why he shouldn't ride into the Alamo?" Captain Kimball shifted his weight in his saddle, raised in his stirrups, and looked at the circle of thirty-two men.

Nobody moved or flinched.

William Summers rubbed his chin and laughed. "I'm the only one here that's been sentenced to die." Summers shook his head and laughed.

CHAPTER X

"Well, it's about 2 a.m. I figure them Mexicans are about as sleepy as they're gonna get." John W. Smith licked his lips and used his fingers to smooth down his handlebar mustache as he eyed Captain Kimball. "You ready for me to do some coyote howlin'?"

Captain Kimball nodded his head.

Smitty pulled in a big lungfull of air, drew back his head, cupped his hands in front of his mouth, and let out one low, mournful coyote howl. "Owoow, owoow, owoow."

Billy looked down at the white walls of the Alamo. He saw the shadows of men running on top of the wall, then saw them disappear into the inner patio.

John Smith nodded his head and smiled. "We got their attention." He turned to Captain Kimball with his black-toothed grin. "I told you I wasn't worth a damn as a coyote howler."

Captain Kimball shifted in his saddle and looked at Smitty. "When're you gonna howl again?"

"I'm gonna wait 'til Crockett gets up on top of that wall."

In a moment, Billy made out the forms of two men walking toward the northeast corner of the Alamo wall. One was much taller than the other, and he looked as if he had on an odd kind of hat, a flat, furry looking hat, maybe a coon-skin hat.

Smitty grinned and pointed his long arm at the two men standing at the corner of the Alamo wall. He threw back his head and let go another low, mournful coyote howl. "Owoow, owoow, owoow, owoow."

Smitty hadn't much more than lowered his head when a coyote howl burst into the night air. It sounded like a real, genuine howl—low and mournful, with some yips right on the end, like a mama coyote telling her pups which way to go.

The men in the circle stared at each other and turned their ears toward the Alamo, listening to see if there would be another coyote howl.

"Owoow, owoow, owoow."

The men leaned their heads, listening for a third coyote howl. None came.

Captain Kimball sighed. "Well, that's our signal. Smitty, you lead the way. Summers, you get up here right in front of me. Everybody else fall in line behind me. Let's go just as fast as we can go. We've got three-quarters of a mile to ride."

Billy mounted Alexander. He reached for his bridle reins and noticed that his left bridle rein was still tied around Comanche's neck.

Smitty had already started his gallop toward the north portal of the Alamo. Summers was right behind him, and Captain Kimball was right behind Summers. Everybody except Billy was galloping down the hill.

The bridle rein was still tied around Comanche's neck! Billy kicked Alexander and he bolted, dragging Comanche by the neck. The rein was too short; it was dragging Comanche!

Billy pulled up on the reins, stopping Alexander. The horsemen were racing down the hill, far ahead of Billy. He piled off his horse and grabbed Comanche, holding him with both hands. He began untying the leather bridle rein, but it was jerked tight. Billy gritted his teeth, jerking at the tight knot. it wouldn't untie!

Billy was on his hands and knees, struggling with the stubborn leather knot. It was tight, too tight for his fingers. It wouldn't untie.

The horsemen were disappearing down the hill. Billy was alone. He jerked out his pocket knife and cut the leather rein above the tight knot. Billy ran his finger under the knot around Comanche's throat. It was tight, but there was room to breathe.

He grabbed Comanche, threw him across the saddle, and climbed on his horse. Alexander stomped his feet and turned his head, looking at Billy, waiting for a kick, waiting for directions.

Billy looked down the hill toward the Alamo. The horsemen were half way to the gate.

Should Billy follow? Was it too late? Should he turn away? To the south, toward home?

Billy lifted Comanche onto the saddle and kicked Alexander and headed toward the northeast portal of the white-walled Alamo.

Comanche jerked and tried to leap down, but Billy tightened his grip around the dog's body, lowering his chin against the dog's head to help hold him. Comanche whined and struggled and tried to jump down again.

"Shut up, Comanche," Billy whispered as he kicked his heels into Alexander's flanks, trying to catch up to the main body of horsemen, who were now far ahead.

Comanche whined and bit softly, unhappily, at Billy's restraining hand. He then kicked at the saddle with all four legs and leaped away, rolling and tumbling in the underbrush beside the trail.

Billy stared at his tumbling dog. "You stinkin' ole Indian dog!" he shouted. Billy rose in his saddle and turned to watch Comanche.

Comanche was now on his feet, racing, not down the same trail that the horses were following, but off to the left.

Billy pulled up on Alexander's reins, trying to stop him. But Alexander had his head down. He was racing toward the other horses that were not far ahead now. Billy thought about turning Alexander to the left, in the direction Comanche was running. Maybe they could run him down and catch him.

Then Billy saw something white running through the tall grass toward the line of horsemen. He squinted his eyes against the racing wind. What was that running toward the line of horsemen? Was it a man? Was it a Mexican soldier?

Then Billy saw a long-barreled rifle aiming in his direction. Whoever it was, he was aiming at Billy. Billy lowered his head down on Alexander's mane and kicked the horse as hard as he could in the flanks. He had his head low and on the left side of Alexander's neck. Then he saw Comanche leap into the air with his forepaws and his white teeth flashing. He hit the Mexican soldier full on the chest, sending him sprawling in the deep grass. Billy couldn't see Comanche any more, but he could hear him growling and biting and tearing. Ahead of him, he saw the dark door of the Alamo swing open as John W. Smith, William Summers and Captain Kimball raced through the open door, followed by the line of horsemen.

Shots began to ring out from the right and from the left. Billy gripped his one long bridle rein and flipped it against Alexander's flanks. He could see that the door ahead of him did seem to grow bigger as he got closer. It now seemed big enough for a wagon to go through. Billy saw a man standing beside the door as he raced through the wooden portal. The man pushed the door shut as Billy and Alexander galloped into the patio of the Alamo.

Billy jumped off Alexander and ran back toward the door, shouting, "Don't close that door! Don't close that door!" He waved his arms and shouted as he ran toward the door.

"Huh? What's that?" The bearded buffalo-coated man at the door looked over his shoulder, staring at Billy. "Is there another man out there?"

"Naw, I'm the last man, but my dog's out there. You

let him in!"

"A dog?" The man stared at Billy, who was now at the door, leaning against it, pushing it open.

"He saved my life! You open that door!" Billy shouted, leaning forward, bracing his legs, pushing the door open.

"Son, there's an awful lot of Mexicans out there." The doorman stepped back and let Billy push the door open.

"Well, there's a few less of 'em. My dog just ate one of 'em."

The big doorman and Billy laughed as Comanche came trotting through the door slowly, head down, his red tongue dripping sweat. Billy grabbed him with both arms and hugged him tight.

"I always heard Indian dogs didn't like Mexicans." Billy grinned as he hugged Comanche.

Courtesy
Daughters of the
Republic of Texas Library,
San Antonio, Texas

CHAPTER XI

"I would like to talk to your men, Sir. I am Colonel Travis." The man saluted Captain Kimball. "I want to meet the kind of men that had the courage, the raw guts, to enter a fort surrounded by 4,000 Mexican soldiers."

"They're men, Sir. They're all men, even if some of 'em look like boys." Captain Kimball placed his hand on the shoulder of a huge man standing beside him. "This here's Albert Martin. He enlisted as a private, but he and I were both elected Captain, so I'm going to call him Captain Martin."

"Where you from?" Travis asked.

"Gonzales," Martin nodded as Travis moved down the line shaking hands and slapping the backs of the dusty arrivals.

Travis stopped at two young men standing side by side. He shook hands with the taller of the two. "You're brothers!" Travis noticed the blond hair straggling out of their hats was the same color.

The taller brother pulled his hand loose from his younger brother's tight grip and shook hands with Travis. "I'm Rupert (Poe) Allen, an' this here's my little brother, James Allen. We call him Jim."

"Mighty glad to have you aboard." Travis paused to study Jim Allen's fuzzy unshaven face. He shook his head and moved on down the line.

"Isaack G. Baker."
"John Blair."
"Robert Brown."
"Freeman H.K. Day."
"John Davis."

"Adolph Devault."
"Jacob Durst."
"George W. Cottle."
"John E. Garvin."
"James George."
"Will Fishbaugh."

Travis was moving down the line when he came to a boy that, standing as tall as he could, still didn't reach as high as the top of Travis' shirt pocket. "Whoa! What have we here? Is this one of your men?" Travis turned to Captain Kimball.

Kimball stared at thin-faced Galba Fuqua. "That's Galba Fuqua. He ain't very big. He ain't tall in the saddle; he's tall in the heart. That boy ain't got no home, but he asked to come. He kept looking at me, no matter how often I shook my head, till finally I just quit shaking my head. He started grinning ever since I said he could go with us."

"Good boy, good boy." Travis patted Galba Fuqua's thin shoulders and continued on down the line.

"John Harris."
"Thomas Jackson."
"David Andrew Kent."

Travis came to Billy King. Billy had his head down, trying to look up through embarrassed eyes.

"What have we here?" Travis stepped close to Billy and raised his forefinger, rubbing it back and forth across Billy's unshaven chin.

"Billy P. King, Sr." Billy tightened his lips and reached up with one hand, feeling of his fuzzy chin.

"Have you ever shaved, Billy P. King?" Travis asked.

Billy stared at Colonel Travis for a helpless instant, then glanced around as his lip trembled. He lowered his chin to his chest and slowly shook his head.

"Where's your gun?" Travis looked at Billy's empty hands.

Billy shrugged and held up both hands. "Pa wouldn't let me have our gun. We didn't have but one."

Travis shook his head, staring at Billy with hands-on-hips disapproval. "An unshaven boy without a gun. What'm I supposed to do, give him a gun or hide him?"

Travis continued on down the line, shaking hands with the men from Gonzales.

"Isaac Millsaps."

Travis shook Isaac's hand. He clung to Isaac's hand long after the shake was over, looking into Millsap's proud blue eyes. He spoke in a low and thoughtful tone. "Isn't your wife—isn't she blind?"

"Yep," Isaac nodded, "Millie's blind, but none of our seven children are."

"Fair enough." Travis nodded and moved on down the line.

"Jesse McCoy."

Travis nodded and moved on.

"Thomas R. Miller."

"The wealthiest man in Gonzales!" Colonel Travis smiled as he shook Tom Miller's hand. "What brought you to the Alamo?" Travis asked.

"I came to watch Johnnie Kellog die." Miller turned his gaze on the man next to him. "I came to watch him die."

"Aw, he's just mad 'cause I stole his wife." Johnnie Kellog jerked his head, riffling his hand through his dark, curly hair. "He's a poor sport. He ain't about to watch Johnnie Kellog die. Miller'll die long before Johnnie Kellog. I borrowed his pretty little red-headed wife, but Miller ain't got the guts to do anythin' about it. If one of us dies first, you can bet it'll be old Tom Miller."

Travis shook his head disapprovingly as he moved on down the line of new arrivals

"Thomas Hendricks."

"Richardson Perry."

"Robert White."

Then Travis stopped and leaned forward, looking into the eyes of another young man. "How old are you, Son?"

"Sixteen." The young man stiffened and straightened his back, reaching for more height. "I'm Johnny Gaston, Sir. I'm Johnnie Kellog's brother-in-law. He said I could come along with him."

Travis shook his head again, then smiled. "At least it looks like you've shaved once or twice."

"Yes, Sir, I sure have. I even brought my razor." He pointed at his saddlebag.

There was one more man in the line. Travis walked toward him with his big hand outstretched.

"I'm W.E. Summers from Pecan Valley." He nodded as he spoke. "Lately from the San Felipe jail." He grinned as Travis shook his hand. "I killed a cotton broker in San Felipe, and the sheriff didn't much want to hang me. He let me outa jail provided I'd come to the relief of the Alamo." Summers grinned. " 'Spect the sheriff figgered I'd die in the Alamo an' save him a hangin'."

"Might just do that." Travis turned and placed his hands on his hips, now speaking to the men gathered around the fire. "We're all gonna die unless we can figure some way for 183 men to whip 4,000 Mexican soldiers just outside those gates."

CHAPTER XII

Captain Kimball led his white palomino, Mad Hatter, to the open bonfire at the north end of the patio. He took off his gloves and warmed his hands at the fire.

"Don't suppose you all got any hot coffee for some cold troupers?" he grinned at Davy Crockett as he warmed his hands.

Crockett's big lean face broke into a gentle smile. "Coffee?" he laughed. "We been outa coffee for a couple of weeks."

"No coffee?" Captain Kimball turned his face to the soldiers standing around the fire. His grin disappeared as he studied the grim faces. "Well," he stuffed his gloves into his hip pocket, "at least you got a warm fire."

"You bring any food? Any groceries?" Crockett asked.

Captain Kimball shook his head.

Crockett spoke, "All we got is shelled corn, beef, and horsemeat. We don't even have salt. We have beef one day, an' for a change of fare, we try horsemeat." He shook his head. "Horsemeat gets a little slick. It sticks in your throat 'fore you can get a belly full."

A tall man in a tan buckskin jacket joined the throng gathered around the fire. The men stepped back and made way for him as he approached the fire.

Crockett leaned on his Kentucky rifle as he nodded toward the new arrival. "Colonel Bowie, this here is Captain Kimball from Gonzales. He just brought in thirty-two men, the first troupers to come to the relief of the Alamo."

Colonel Bowie nodded and stepped toward Captain Kimball. He shook his hand, patting him on the back.

"I'm well-acquainted with George Kimball. He's known throughout Texas as the 'Mad-Hatter' of Gonzales. You brought some volunteers to relieve this garrison of weary, hungry men. How many troupers did you bring?" Bowie glanced around the fire, looking about him, appraising the new faces.

"We brought all the able-bodied men we could find. Three Taylor brothers from Liberty, William Summers and two other jail birds from San Felipe, and twenty-six men from Gonzales. Thirty-two men in all." Captain Kimball stiffened his shoulders and waved his arm proudly at the young faces gathered around the fire.

"Thirty-two men!" Colonel Bowie glared at Billy King. "You mean three towns only furnished thirty-two volunteers?" He stepped toward Billy King and ran his fingers across Billy's chin. "Three jail birds from San Felipe, three brothers from Liberty, and freckle-faced, half-grown kids that ain't never felt a razor. They don't look like troupers to me." He ran his finger under Billy's chin again, feeling of the unshaven fuzz and shaking his head. Then he noticed Billy had no gun. "Where's your gun, Son? Don't tell me you rode into the Alamo without a gun."

Billy nodded his head. "Pa wouldn't let me take the gun."

Bowie turned his head in disgust. "Fuzzy cheeks and no gun. Great relief column!"

"But Colonel," Davy Crockett cradled his rifle in one arm and stretched his long legs off the edge of the burro cart in the patio, "these men came in tonight. This means other men may be on the way. Some more may come in tonight, maybe tomorrow."

Colonel Bowie pounded the palm of his hand against the long knife at his belt. "General Santa Anna rode in eight days ago with four thousand soldiers and fourteen cannons and we've sent out three messengers asking for relief, and all the response we get is thirty-two men from three towns, and most of them ain't men and some of them don't even have guns." He scowled at Billy King as he spoke.

"I can shoot a cannon," Billy volunteered.

"Did you bring any cannon shells?" Colonel Travis spoke quickly and cut him off sharply.

Billy shook his head and watched as Colonel Travis walked up to the men at the fire.

"What we need is men, men with guns." Colonel Travis tossed his disapproving glance at Billy King. "And we could use a wagon-load of cannon shells. We got the cannons, but not enough shells." The Commander of the Almo sighed and placed his hand on Billy's shoulder. Billy cut his eye and studied Travis' big hand as the Colonel spoke.

"Well lad, you're here, and I have to commend you for the guts you showed, coming in here without even having a gun to defend yourself. I'll assign you to Sergeant Ward. He can use a little extra help with that eighteen-pound cannon up on the southwest revetment. He needs a match boy, and when you ain't helping him, you can chase down these four-, eight- and twelve-pound cannon shells Santa Anna's cannons are lobbing in here. We have to chase down their cannon shells so we'll have something to shoot back at them." He slapped Billy on the shoulder. "You hop up there to the biggest cannon in the Alamo. You'll find it at the top of the revetment at the southwest corner of this patio. Tell Sergeant Ward I sent you, and stay there even if he gets drunk and runs you away."

CHAPTER XIII

"Your name is Billy King, eh, and you got here without a gun, eh?" The gruff and mustachioed giant of a man slapped Billy King on the shoulder. "Well my name's Billy, too. My full name is William Daniel Ward. Everybody calls me the Irishman, 'cause I'm an Irishman an' I'm always drinking Irish whiskey, and damn proud of the fact."

Sergeant Ward had huge cracked hands. He had a face like a mustachioed English bulldog. His broken nose was mashed up against his face. His lips were so thick they almost bent over and touched his chin. He had a mustache like a Norseman. It started off dark at his lips, but it lightened and got grayish-white at the tips.

"You got a hole in your ear." Billy pointed at the round hole in the top of Sergeant Ward's left ear.

"Yeh," Sergeant Ward felt of the hole in his left ear, "that's a little momento of a French bullet at Waterloo. I got a hole shot in my ear, and another shot in my ass." Sergeant Ward reached back and patted his butt. "When me and the Duke of Wellington whopped Napoleon at the Battle of Waterloo."

"Were you really at Waterloo?" Billy asked.

"Yeah, Son, I was at Waterloo. That weren't so long ago—only twenty-one years. It don't seem long ago to me, not a'tall."

"Are you really a cannoneer?" Billy asked.

"Am I a cannoneer!" Sergeant Ward shifted the cud of chewing tobacco in his mouth and spat, hitting the bottom spoke of the right wheel of the eighteen-pound cannon. "I was dragging cannons around Europe before you was ever born."

"Will you teach me how to shoot a cannon?"

Sergeant Ward turned his head and glanced over the wall toward the Mexican lines. "I don't know whether we'll have time or not." He spat over the wall. "It'd take two years for me to teach you what I know about cannons." He stood at the rear of the cannon, between the wheels, shutting one eye and glancing down the barrel. He leaned over and patted the copper button at the rear of the cannon. "Well, you're my match boy, my cannon boy. I guess I'd better start teaching you something. In the first place, cannoneers don't call cannons 'cannons.' We call our cannons 'guns,' and we take care of 'em real careful-like, like a woman protectin' her glass mirror. We're mighty particular who touches our cannons, and especially where they touch our cannons. They's some men can't bring nothin' but bad luck."

"Do you aim with these handles?" Billy leaned over and grasped the handles that jutted out on each side of the cannon barrel.

Sergeant Ward shook his head. "Them ain't handles." Sergeant Ward had his hands on his hips. "They're called dolphins, and that's 'cause the first handles put on the side of a cannon barrel were cast in the shape of a fish. And we do use them like handles to wheel and push and pull a cannon back into position after firing."

Sergeant Will Ward was a hairy bear of a man, six-foot three and two hundred twenty-five pounds. Huge curls of iron-gray hair folded out from underneath a soot-covered black hat, which was pulled down so low on his head that his hairy cauliflowered ears stuck out like huge deformed mushrooms. Billy thought the ear with the bullet hole in it looked neater and cleaner than the one that didn't have the hole in it. The Sergeant had the burned-sulphur odor of gunpowder, especially on his right side, where he now wore the heavy black gunner's glove. His left arm had a long saber scar. His right arm had a tattoo of a cannon with a cannonball and powder coming out the muzzle of the cannon.

Billy stared at the cannon and cannonball on Sergeant Ward's arm. He rubbed it with his forefinger and noticed it didn't come off. He looked up at Sergeant Ward. "That's a tattoo, isn't it?" Billy asked.

Sergeant Ward nodded.

"Does it wash off?"

"I wouldn't know. I never tried." Sergeant Ward gave Billy a long, dry look. Then a smile broke across his thick lips. "It don't wash off, Mr. King. That dye was planted under the skin with a needle.

"A needle!" Billy squeezed his eyes and wrinkled his nose.

"Know any other way of gettin' a liquid dye under your skin?"

Billy shook his head. Then he looked up at Sergeant Ward. "I don't wanna be tattooed with no needle."

"That hot cannon barrel'll burn a few tattoos into you. When you get to shootin' a cannon fast-like, it gets bloody hot, your hand'll slip and you'll burn your arm. When the fightin' gets fierce around here, you'll let your hand slip and touch that cannon barrel with your arm. You'll be tattooed before it's over."

Billy pointed at the cannon tattooed on Sergeant Ward's arm. "Will I have a tattoo like that?"

Sergeant Ward shook his head. "Naw, burn tattoos don't look very pr'tty." Sergeant Ward pointed at the white welts around both forearms. "Most cannon barrel burns just leave a white scar where the hot metal cooked a little flesh. A good cannoneer can fire a cannon ever' two and a half minutes, providin' he don't take too long aimin'. But after eight or ten shots, a cannon barrel gets so hot, you can't put gun powder in it. It'll blow up before you can ram it home, despite sponging out the barrel with a wet sponge after every shot."

"How do you get burned?" Billy asked.

"Well now, Billy, when you're in a hot fight, with three to five men to each cannon, that cannon barrel's still got to be handled lots of times. First, you clean it out. You've got to get all the pieces of linen that packed your gun powder. You got to get it out of there. Then you've got to sponge it out, and you've got to clean your vent hole. Then you gotta ram your powder cartridges into the rear of that cannon and ram your patch next to your powder. Then you put your ball in there, and then you have to ram home your gromet to hold that cannon ball in place tightly against the powder. Then you have to wheel that cannon back up into firing position. Then when it's fired, the crew's got to hang onto that cannon with ropes and staves to keep it from recoiling over the wall. And all the time you're servicing a cannon, you're gonna be touchin' that hot barrel." Sergeant Ward grinned and touched the leather glove on his right hand. "That's why old experienced gunners wear gloves."

"Tell me about cannons, Sergeant Ward. This is the first cannon I ever saw in my life."

"You wanna know about cannons, do you Son?" Sergeant Ward took his powder cloth and began rubbing and polishing the dolphin handles on the sides of the eighteen-pound cannon. "Well, I reckon you have a right to know. I don't know how I ever learned without asking questions. A German monk, Bertholdschwarz, of Freburk, Germany, invented the first cannon in 1313."

"But didn't the Chinese . . ." Billy interrupted.

"No, Billy, the Chinese didn't invent cannons. They invented rockets. They used 'em as incendiaries, but they didn't do anything but catch forts on fire. They did invent gun powder, and they used it to fire rockets. But their rockets never exploded. They were made of wood and paper and didn't do any damage where they hit. Some count in Florence, Italy, ordered the first metal cannon in 1326."

"More'n five hundred years ago!" Billy exclaimed.

Sergeant Ward nodded his head. "Yeah, after five hundred years, we still make cannons just about like they did that first one. The first one was made out of copper sheeting covered with leather. Now we cast them out of bronze or iron. About the only improvement that's been made in cannons is that we've improved gun powder. The Chinese gun powder was a fine powder that fired alright, but if you carried it around, it tended to separate. The sulphur and saltpetre and charcoal separated. The sulphur, bein' the heaviest, it went to the bottom. And the charcoal bein' the lightest, it rose to the top, especially if you carried it or bounced it around. Then when you got it to the battlefield, it wouldn't shoot." Sergeant Ward grinned through his heavy mustache. "If you wanted dependable gun powder, you had to mix it on the battlefield while you's gettin' shot at. Then some bright lad noticed that when you dried out wet gun powder, it had a tendancy to flake and turn into flakes bigger'n wheat. When it dried out, it stayed in them big flakes, and the sulphur, saltpetre, and charcoal stayed together. Then when you shot it, you had much better gun powder, because it didn't tend to pack so tightly that air couldn't get in there to help give it a sharp explosion. That's why we have three types of gun powder. We use the fine grain powder for priming the cannon. We use the small grain powder for the smaller cannons. And we use the large grain gun powder for the heavier cannons, to shoot a shell as big as an eighteen-pounder."

"Gee, shootin' a cannon's a lot more complicated than I thought." Billy looked at the heavy eighteen-pounder with awed eyes.

"Years ago, when I was a young cannoneer like you, we used to think whatever weight of cannon ball you fired, you had to have the same weight of gun powder. Now we know it doesn't take the same weight." Sergeant Ward slapped the cannon barrel with his open palm.

"This eighteen-pounder doesn't use eighteen pounds of powder. It uses twelve. We make our powder last a little longer, and our cannon balls go just as far." Sergeant Ward grinned at Billy's eager blue eyes. "They ain't much to shootin' a cannon here in the Alamo,' 'cause you can see what you're shootin' at. When you can see what you're shootin' at, that's what we call layin' a gun in line of sight. That's where you look right down the barrel and see what you're shootin' at. Them Mexicans ain't far enough away for us to have to shoot over somethin' and hope it comes down on somebody we wanna hit."

"You mean you just aim this barrel right at a Mexican soldier and fire it?" Billy asked.

"Naw, it ain't quite that simple, Mr. King."

"Gee, I wish you'd show me how to shoot a cannon."

"Well, mostly aimin' comes as a matter of experience. You have to figger how high you are off the ground, how much powder you've got in the chamber, the weight of your ball, how strong the wind is, and what direction the wind's blowin'." Sergeant Ward grinned. "And you never hit what you're shootin' at. The best you do is just hit close to what you're shootin' at and hope it'll bounce pieces and splinters around an' get something."

"Just how do you aim a cannon, anyway?" Billy asked.

"Well, these are field pieces. That means you have to turn the barrel to the direction you want it to go, to right or left. Then you raise or lower the barrel. Most cannons have an elevating screw you turn to raise or lower the barrel. But this ole eighteen-pounder got its elevatin' screw broke. We have to use wedges. You pound a wedge in underneath the elevation block to raise the barrel till you've got it aimed high enough or low enough to hit what you're shootin' at."

"Oh, I see." Billy nodded. "Is that what that hammer's for?" He pointed at the heavy, black-handled hammer lying across the trail just below the butt end of the cannon.

"Yeah, that't the wedge hammer."

"How do you turn it from right to left?" Billy asked.

"A cannon has to be turned real gentle-like. We generally have a man on each wheel and somebody at the rear, swingin' that trail. That trail's got to be well-anchored so it won't jump off the wall in the recoil. Then I use wedges to raise or lower the barrel till I've got it aimed just like I want it."

Billy nodded.

"Sergeant, tell me one thing. Why is there a bucket of water at each one of these cannons?" Billy leaned toward the eighteen-pounder and gently kicked the metal bucket of water that was sitting on the ground near the mouth of the eighteen pound cannon.

"Oh, that's a swabber's bucket. You have to swab out a cannon after ever' shot with a wet swab." Sergeant Ward shook his head. "That cannon barrel's gotta be powerful clean and cool if it's gonna work right and if you don't want it to explode."

"Explode!" Billy gasped.

Sergeant Ward nodded his head. "Cannons explode all the time."

"What causes a cannon to explode?"

"Cannons explode when they're not properly cared for. You've never seen a battle yet where there was artillery used where some damn fool didn't try to fire a cannon too fast and load it while it was too hot and have the powder explode."

"I still don't understand what causes a cannon to explode. Will you explain it to me, Sergeant?"

"Well now, Billy Boy, let's just say we was in a battle, and the enemy was runnin' at us with their bayonettes flashing in the sun, and we decided not to clean out that cannon barrel after ever' shot. Say you was handlin' the ramrod, and you rammed a packet of gunpowder back to the breech of the gun without first cleanin' that barrel out and coolin' it off with a wet swab. You had your gun powder back at the breech, but you hadn't charged it with your vent powder. You were charging your gun with your cannon shell. You had it right in the breech, but you hadn't pushed it back against the powder. That barrel's shot, there's a spark of flame back there against your gunpowder." Sergeant Ward shut his eyes. He wrinkled his face in an ominous frown. "When that gunpowder explodes and there ain't no cannon shell stuck up against that gunpowder, you don't have the firing of a cannon shell; you have an explosion of a cannon barrel. It's like shootin' a cannon barrel that's been stopped up by mud. That cannon barrel explodes in your face. An exploding cannon barrel is a lot more destructive than a cannon shell. That's how an artilleryman destroys his cannon when he has to fall back and can't take his cannon with him. He destroys it to keep the enemy from being able to use it after he runs."

"You mean that bucket of water is that important?" Billy asked.

Sergeant Ward nodded. "That water is what keeps a cannon working for you against your enemies instead of turning into your own enemy. If you shoot a cannon without cleaning the barrel out after ever' shot to make sure there's no flannel cloth or unfired gunpowder, and you stick another packet of gunpowder in that barrel, it'll blow up on you. To keep it from being dangerous, we swab that barrel down with a wet swab. And it's that wet swab what makes that cannon ready to fire again."

"You mean you can fire a cannon right after you swab it down with a wet swab?" Billy asked. He put his hands on each side of the cannon muzzle and stared down the cannon barrel. "It looks like the water would keep the cannon from shooting."

"The heat in the cannon barrel evaporates water faster'n you can blink an eye."

"Oh." Billy looked at Sergeant Ward for a thoughtful instant. "Have you ever blew up your own cannon?"

"You mean have I ever spiked a cannon?" the Sergeant asked.

Billy nodded.

Sergeant Ward sighed. "I've spiked more cannons than I like to remember."

"Ain't that cowardly to blow up your own cannon?"

"Spiking a cannon is cowardly, yes, my boy, but it is also the most dangerous thing a man has to do."

"Handling a cannon sounds like a lot of fun." Billy smiled and rubbed his hands along the barrel of the big cannon.

"You know, I might make a cannoneer out of you yet."

"Sergeant Ward, how far does a cannon shell go? How far does it sink into a fort?" Billy asked in a quiet moment.

"Son, you're wonderin' why them Mexican shells bounce off'n our walls, ain't yuh?"

Billy nodded. "Yeah, an' I see our shells sink into their adobe walls and just, just disappear."

"Neither one of us is doin' much damage to the other, Billy boy. Is that what you're wonderin', what you're askin' about?"

"Yeah. Why do our cannon shells sink into adobe brick sort of like droppin' a rock down a well? An' why do their shells bounce off our stone walls?"

"The French wondered about that, son, and back in 1834 at Metz, France, them French they ran a test. They not only tested cannons, they even tested muskets—muzzle-loading rifles like Crockett an' them Tennessee mountain boys shoot."

"What'd they find? What'd they find out?"

"Well, for one thing they found that our stone walls was the toughest things you can shoot at. An eighteen-pounder like this 'un here only goes an inch an' a half into a thick stone wall, an' this is the biggest gun in San Antonio. It's bigger'n any piece them Mexicans got.

They got lots of twelve- and eight-pounders, but they didn't try to drag no eighteen-pounders across the desert of death, as they call the Cactus Desert southwest of here. Bowie calls it "Wild Horse" Desert, 'cause he used to catch wild horses out there where there ain't much water. Anyway, the French shot cannon shells at dirt walls, an' they found this ole eighteen-pounder at four hundred yards went sixty inches, or somethin' like five feet, into a dirt embankment. Didn't do no damage; it just went in and went in and went in." Sergeant Ward eyed Billy. "You get the message? Cannon shells bounce off thick stone walls and they disappear into dirt walls."

"What about our north wall? Ain't the stone on our north wall kinda thin?"

"Shush!" Sergeant Ward put his powder-blackened finger to his lips. "We're hopin' them Mexicans don't know about how thin that north wall is."

"Didn't the Mexicans build the Alamo?" Billy asked.

"Yeah, they built it," Sergeant Ward grinned, "but maybe they forgot that north wall ain't but ten to twelve inches thick!"

Billy shook his head.

Sergeant Ward patted the black barrel of his eighteen-pound cannon. "This here eighteen-pounder'll shoot nearly fourteen inches into concrete at four hundred yards, an' it'll go thirty-four inches into solid oak." He turned and pointed at Davy Crockett and his Tennessee Volunteers at the pallisade of logs and dirt-filled hides between the chapel and the south wall. "Them long-barrelled muskets will go three inches into oak at fifty yards and only one inch at three hundred yards. They'll go nine inches into dirt at fifty yards, and four inches at three hundred yards."

"I wish I had one of them muskets." Billy licked his lips as he looked at Crockett leaning against his long-barrelled Kentucky rifle.

"Don't you go talkin' like that, Billy Boy. They ain't

nothin' one of them Kentucky rifles can do that this ole eighteen-pounder can't do better."

"It don't shoot as straight," Billy quickly corrected him.

"It don't have to," Sergeant Ward grinned. "It'll blow a man down if it gets in ten inches of him."

Billy walked away, leaning over, feeling of Comanche's ears. "Sometimes I think Comanche'll kill more Mexicans than that smelly ole cannon."

Courtesy
Daughters of the
Republic of Texas Library,
San Antonio, Texas

CHAPTER XIV

It was dark. Sergeant Ward raised his red clay jug to his lips and leaned his head backward, shaking the jug. He held it away from him upside down. Not even a drop fell out.

"You drink whiskey?" Billy asked. "That ain't good for you, is it? Your jug's nearly empty."

"Don't worry about Will Ward. When I run outta tequila, they ain't no walls gonna stop or slow me down. When I'm lookin' for a full keg of tequila, I'll just borrow Juan Seguin's big black sombrero and drop quietly over that south wall. I'll march into San Antonio with a little gold piece between my teeth. I'll lay it on the counter and walk out with a fresh keg of tequila. And nobody'll stop me."

"They won't?" Billy King asked.

"They ain't nobody out there u'd stop me an' nobody in this fort that would try to stop me."

"Not even Jim Bowie?" Billy asked.

"Not even Jim Bowie. Me and him done had one fight. We broke up three chairs, one bench, and a crock of tequila."

"He didn't whup you?"

"Nope, and I didn't whup him. We stood there and fought like a coupla stud horses tearin' up the country over a pretty mare an' neither one of us doin' any good."

"Well what happened?" Billy asked.

"We'd done fought till we was bloody well tuckered out. I'd done broke two chairs over his head, and he'd done broke one chair and a wooden bench over my head. We were both gettin' sobered up and were beginning to stand there and huff and puff and stare at each other. Then this feller Crockett come in there. First thing he did was pick up my crock of tequila and drop it on that stone floor. I quit fightin' Bowie and started for Crockett. He just stood there and laughed at me." Sergeant Ward let a big grin break across his bristled cheeks. "First thing you know, we was all three laughin'."

"Shortly after my fight with Jim Bowie, he broke his back." Sergeant Ward shook his head.

"He did?" Billy asked. "How'd he do it? Wrestling Davy Crockett?"

"Nope," Sergeant Ward's face remained grim, "he was mounting a cannon on top o' the shed on the south wall the day Santa Anna's troops arrived. That shed's roofed with rotten cottonwood logs. One of the cannon wheels caved through a rotten log. It rolled to the side quicklike an' that cannon barrel struck Bowie, it crushed his chest an' broke his back. He's been stretcher bound ever since. Can't walk 'er stand," Sergeant Ward grinned, "but ole Jim Bowie's got his pistols an' that man-eatin' knife. He'll take a passel o' Mexicans 'fore they git him."

"I never shot a cannon. You think I'll ever get to shoot one?" Billy asked.

Sergeant Ward frowned and scratched behind his left ear. His frown deepened as he raised both hands and felt of his long mustache. His hands stopped when his fingertips got to the tips of his mustache. "Well, I don't know. We're powerfully short on cannon shells, or I'd let you shoot one right now."

"You would!" Billy exclaimed.

Sergeant Ward nodded, clamping his teeth together in an English bulldog grimmace. He raised up, turned, and stared over the wall toward the Mexican lines. Then he turned back to Billy. "The next Mexican cannon shell that gets lobbed in here, you go run it down and bring it to me and I'll let you shoot it back at them."

"You use Mexican cannon shells?" Billy asked, looking at the triangular pile of cannon shells neatly stacked near the trail.

"We damn well do," Sergeant Ward laughed. "If we didn't run down their cannon shells, we would already be out of shells." Sergeant Ward leaned over and pointed at the dents in the round cannon shells piled in triangles beside the twelve-pound cannon further down the wall.

"You mean if I run down a cannon shell and bring it back, you'll let me shoot it?"

"That's what I said."

Billy walked over to the wall and placed his arms over the wall. He stared to the west toward the Mexican lines. "When are they gonna fire one of their cannons?"

"They're having their siesta right now. It's about over. They take about an hour- or two-hour nap right after their noon meal. And General Santa Anna don't want no cannons hot while he's having his siesta, you can bet on that."

"That sounds like a good time to shoot a cannon." Billy ran and bent over the rear of the cannon, aiming down the barrel. Then he leaned over to the left side of the barrel and stared at a tiny copper hole in the gun barrel right at the breech. "This cannon's got a hole in it!" Billy exclaimed, pointing at the copper-reamed hole.

"That's the vent hole," Sergeant Ward laughed as he polished the copper vent hole with his forefinger. "Every cannon's got a vent hole. You can't shoot a cannon till you fill that vent hole full of powder. Then when you want to shoot the cannon after it has been powdered and charged, you set a fire match to that vent hole." Sergeant Ward slapped his two big hands together with an explosion. "Boom!" He put his big lips together in a slow whistle. "Your cannon fires."

"Oh, I see now." Billy walked around to the muzzle of the cannon, put his finger inside, and wiped away some of the black powder. He smelled of it for an instant, then stuck his hand in the barrel. "You stick your powder in, then you pack it, and you stick your cannon shell in and pack it, and then you charge it with powder at the vent hole. And then when you set a match to that powder, the cannon goes off."

"That's right, Son. You're learnin' fast; that's how you shoot a cannon."

A cannon belched on the Mexican side of the San Antonio River. Billy hunckered his head down into his shoulders and leaned forward and put his fingers to his ears as he heard the whistle of an incoming cannon shell.

Billy shut one eye and grinned at Sergeant Ward, "Santa Anna's siesta must be over." He shut both eyes as the shell hit the Alamo.

The shell hit the west wall, bounced up into the air in a cloud of dust and rock fragments, and fell to earth inside the horse corral.

"That looks like a twelve-pounder." Sergeant Ward pointed at the cannon shell as it rolled out of the dust, sending horses scurrying out of its way. The shell rolled to the east wall of the horse corral, climbed the wall about a foot, then fell to the ground and lay still.

"There's you a cannon shell, Billy Boy. Go bring me that shell and we'll shoot it back at them Mexicans."

Billy took off running.

Sergeant Ward cupped his hands around his mouth. "Don't pick it up with your hands, Billy Boy. It'll still be hot," he warned as Billy raced down off the west wall.

Billy came racing up the reventment tossing the hot cannon ball from hand to hand. "It's hot!" he shouted as he tossed it back and forth, then rolled it in a quick roll toward the triangle of cannon shells near the trail of the huge eighteen-pound cannon at the top of the revetment.

The battered cannon shell rolled and came to a slow stop. Billy picked it up and blew on it. "It's still hot." He tossed the cannon shell from his left hand to his right hand as he studied the husky mustachioed cannoneer with a smile. "It ain't as big as your cannon shells." Billy compared it to the larger shells at Sergeant Ward's eighteen-pound cannon.

Sergeant Ward grabbed the cannon shell from Billy's hands. "That's a little twelve-pounder." He hefted the warm cannon shell, rubbing it between his two huge blackened hands as he grinned at his young cannon boy. "We'll have to trot this li'l twelve-pounder down the wall to Lieutenant Almeron Dickerson's twelve pounder." The huge Sergeant grinned as he rubbed the black gunpowder off the lead cannon shell. "You still want to shoot a cannon shell at Santa Anna?" the Sergeant asked.

"You bet I do!" Billy lifted the cannon shell out of Sergeant Ward's black hands. "Where's ole Santa Anna's tent?" Billy ran to the stone wall and leaned his chin over the cold stone wall.

"Can't quite reach his tent from here." Sergeant Ward placed his hands on the back of Billy's shoulders and aimed him with shoulder shoves toward two pretty white tents with a neat green door folded back, well to the rear of the smaller white soldiers' tents pitched ten yards apart on the west side of the San Antonio River, shimmering its greenish water between the whitish limestone banks of the quiet river.

"Can't shoot Santa Anna?" Billy turned his blond head toward Sergeant Ward.

"Nope, little cannon boy, don't believe we got a cannon in the Alamo that'll reach General Santa Anna's green and white tent on the hill."

"Aw shucks." Billy leaned over the wall, clutching his cannon shell against his chest. "I don't wanna waste my cannon shell 'lessen I can land it right in General Santa Anna's pajama pocket." He stared at the quiet white tents with their green silk doors folded back over the white walls.

"I'm sorry, Billy Boy, but if we had a cannon that'd reach Santa Anna's tent over there high on the hill across the river, I reckon ole Sergeant Ward 'ud done pot-shot General Santa Anna and done ended this here war."

Billy stepped back away from the wall, clutching his cannon shell to his chest. "I don't want to shoot my cannon shell 'lessen I can get least a Mexican General." He shook his head, holding his cannon shell tight against his chest.

"I'm sorry." Sergeant Ward stepped away from the Alamo wall. "If my eighteen-pounder can't reach Santa Anna, I know your twelve-pounder can't range his tent."

"I wanna shoot it an' see." Billy held out his cannon shell. "I wanna aim it an' shoot it myself an' see if it'll range far enough."

"Aye." Sergeant Ward nodded. "Maybe you can drop it right in his tent, right in Santa Anna's lap. Never can tell about cannon shells."

"Where can I shoot it?" Billy held the cannon shell up high.

"If you want to shoot at Santa Anna's tent, you'll have to climb down off the wall, cross the patio, stay inside the pallisade, then into the chapel, and climb the stone steps to the roof and use Lieutenant Dickerson's twelve-pounder on the roof of the chapel. I think the parapet atop the roof of the northwest corner of the chapel should give you the best shot at Santa Anna's tent. You wanna take your cannon shell up there?"

Billy nodded, holding his cannon shell with both hands.

"Let's go, lad. Let's drop that shell in Santa Anna's lap."

They raced down the revetment of the eighteen-pounder at the northwest corner of the fort, past the guardhouse, past the northwest portal, past Jim Bowie's room immediately west of the portal, across the northwest corner of the patio, into the west door to the chapel, up the stone stairs to the parapet for Lieutenant Dickerson's twelve-pounder.

"Lieutenant, this here's Billy G. King, one o' the volunteers from Gonzales. He's handlin' the powder match on my eighteen-pounder. I'm teachin' him to be a cannon boy. He ran down one o' Santa Anna's twelve-pound cannon shells, an' now he wants to shoot it back at thu Mexicans. He wants to drop it on Santa Anna's tent, right in his pajama pocket if he can."

Lieutenant Dickerson nodded his head wearily, pushing back his hat. "I've heard of the Cannon Boy from Gonzales." He waved his hand. "Glad to have you aboard." He motioned Billy and Sergeant Ward to take charge of his cannon that was nearest the San Antonio River. "We've dropped shells within fifty yards of his tent, but we can't quite range it. You want me to load it?" Lieutenant Dickerson pushed back his curly black hair as he reached for Billy's cannon ball.

Billy looked at Sergeant Ward. "I wish you'd load it for me." He handed the shell to Sergeant Ward. "I want you to load it, but let me aim it."

Sergeant Ward took Billy's cannon shell and hefted it in the palm of one hand. "Aye now, let's come alive!" he shouted at Lieutenant Dickerson's gunners. "Make that piece ready." He pointed at Dickerson's twelve-pounder.

"It's ready, Sir." Henry Warnell flipped his ramrod in a flashy "Queen Anne" salute. "It's loaded an' ready to fire."

"Oh." Sergeant Ward stiffened his shoulders and stopped hefting Billy's cannon shell. He lowered the cannon shell. "Right you are. Your cannon should always be loaded an' ready." He lowered Billy's cannon shell some more and stared at it. "But we don't want to shoot Lieutenant Dickerson's cannon shell." He wiggled Billy's cannon shell. "We want to shoot this 'un, Billy boy's cannon shell. My cannon boy wants to shoot his own cannon shell, one he chased down so he can shoot it back at them Mexicans.

"This cannon's already charged. It'll have to be fired 'fore you can put another shell in it." Lieutenant Dickerson folded his arms.

"That's right." Sergeant Ward nodded his head sadly. "You don't unload a charged cannon. It's like a musket; once it's loaded, they ain't but one way to unload it, an' that's to shoot." Sergeant Ward patted Billy's cannon shell.

"An' we haven't got 'nuff shells to go wastin' any." Lieutenant Dickerson took off his hat and shaded his eyes as he looked over the walled parapet at the Mexicans on the west side of the river.

"That's right," Sergeant Ward agreed as he hefted Billy's cannon shell. "Nobody but a drunk Irishman 'ud try to unload a charged cannon," he grinned as he laid Billy's battered cannon shell on the ground. "I'm gonna take your shell outa your cannon an' put Billy boy's shell in there." The Sergeant gave the Lieutenant an arrogant slow stare.

"But Sergeant," Lieutenant Dickerson stepped back from the wall, "you know that cannon's liable to blow your head off if'n you try to unload after it's charged."

"Yep." Sergeant Ward stepped toward the muzzle of the cannon. "A couple o' you lads raise that trail while I run a cat scraper in there an pull that rope grommet out." He raised the long-handled bore scraper and measured its length against the outside of the barrel. Then he leaned over the wall and fed the scraper into the muzzle of the cannon. "If it fires while I'm fishing for the grommet that holds the shell agin' the powder," Sergeant Ward grunted as he turned the long wooden handle of the barrel scraper, "if it farts while I got both hands in the muzzle," he tightened his lips and grunted as he twisted the metal scraper deeper and deeper into the cannon, "it'll be this metal-tipped scraper tipping a spark agin' some loose powder." He lowered his head and stared straight down into the barrel of the cannon. He gritted his teeth. "Ah, there it is. I got the grommet; it's comin' out." He looked at Billy. "An' that cannon shell's rollin' out right behind it." He pushed his head around the muzzle of the cannon and shouted at Henry Warnell and John Crane. "Raise that trail; raise it high; keep that cannon shell rollin'." He pulled the scraper out of the cannon, grabbed the rope grommet, stuck the grommet under his arm, and held his fingers against the muzzle until the cannon shell rolled out into his fingers. "There it is!" He grasped the cannon shell and handed it to Billy. "Give Lieutenant Dickerson his precious cannon shell and give me your shell. I'll ram it in here an' fasten it snug against the powder with this grommet, an' your cannon'll be ready to aim."

Sergeant Ward kissed the shell when Billy handed it to him. "Down with the trail. Get this barrel pointing up agin," he shouted at Warnell and Crane. The cannon barrel rose slowly into the sky as the gunners lowered the trail at the rear of the cannon. Sergeant Ward pushed the shell into the cannon. He took the ramrod from Lieutenant Dickerson and pushed the shell to the rear of the cannon, tapped the ramrod gently, and then tapped it again gently. Then he pulled the ramrod out, reached under his arm for the grommet, a ring of rope that slid perfectly down the inside of the cannon barrel, and pushed it to the rear till it was snug against the cannon shell. He tapped the ramrod gently and pulled it out slowly. He turned to Lieutenant Dickerson. "Who says you can't unload and re-load a charged cannon?"

"Drunk Irishmen." Lieutenant Dickerson grinned. "Drunk Irishmen can get away with it when a cannon barrel's cool. If that barrel had been hot, it'd blown your head off."

"A drunk Irishman can do anything."

"But you ain't drunk." Henry Warnell grabbed Sergeant Ward's wool shirt and sniffed close to the Sergeant's mouth.

Sergeant Ward shoved him away. "That's why I stuck my head in the barrel of a charged cannon. I'm sober as a Senorita, an' I don't like it." He wiggled his face unhappily.

"Can I aim it?" Billy asked.

Sergeant Ward nodded his head.

Billy leaned forward and bent over, staring at the cannon. He reached out with one hand, but didn't touch anything. He raised up and looked helplessly at Sergeant Ward. "I can't load a cannon." He shook his head. "I can't even aim one." He puckered his lips and felt them begin to tremble. He held his hands out. "How do you aim a cannon?"

"It's easy, boy." Sergeant Ward slapped Billy briskly on the shoulder, slapping away any chance for a tear to form in Billy's eye. "Tain't nothin' to it. See this here elevating screw at the rear of the cannon, underneath the breech." He pointed at a polished bronze ring underneath the rear of the cannon. "You raise and lower the muzzle with this ring to raise or lower your aim. Then you signal Warnell and Crane to swing that trail around till you have that barrel pointed in the direction you want it to shoot. When you get that barrel pointed at Santa Anna's tent and you fiddle with that elevating screw till you think your shell'll drop right in Santa Anna's lap. Then you step back and get your powder match sparked and lit, you blow on it for good luck, an' when you touch it to that vent hole!" Sergeant Ward shut his eyes and slapped his hands together, "then it's goodbye Santa Anna!"

Billy held up his right hand to direct Henry Warnell, and his left hand to signal John Crane as they gently moved the trail to the right, then to the left. Then Billy held up both hands. The gunners gently lowered the trail and set their shoulder spikes behind the trail to dig into the stone floor of the parapet. Billy shut one eye as he aimed down the long barrel of the cannon while he turned the elevating screw, gently raising the barrel, lowering it, raising it, squinting down the barrel. He raised his hand and touched the screw gently, then raised both hands. He turned to Sergeant Ward. "Where's that powder match?"

Lieutenant Dickerson pressed the cork match against the smoldering fuse and raised it toward his head. He blew on it, and the match glowed. He looked at Sergeant Ward. Sergeant Ward nodded. Lieutenant Dickerson handed the glowing match to Billy. Billy blew on it and grinned as it flamed. "I blew on it for good luck, now you blow on it." Sergeant Ward blew. Billy held the match high. Then he touched the match to the copper-colored vent hole that Sergeant Ward pointed his finger at.

Henry Warnell and John Crane shouldered their heavy metal spikes and shoved them forward into the ground behind the cannon trail to steady the cannon. They shut their eyes as they grunted and steadied the rear of the cannon.

Billy touched the powder match to the black powder spilling out the vent hole.

The cannon belched in a wild roar and jumped forward and then backward. Billy shut his eyes and leaped backward, falling to his knees at Sergeant Ward's feet. He lay there looking up at Sergeant Ward. Sergeant Ward's heavy bearded head was tucked into his neck. His eyes raised and moved upward, following the path of the moving cannon shell. His head jerked. Billy heard the cannon shell crash to earth. Sergeant Ward's head bounced as his eyes followed the path of the cannon shell after it hit. His head bounced again. Gently. Then his Irish face broke into a grin. He glanced down at Billy and shook his head as he grinned.

"Beginner's luck! You hit it!" Sergeant Ward shouted as he clapped his hands together. He reached down and pulled Billy to his feet and pointed his shoulders at the collapsing tent. "You knocked down Santa Anna's tent with your first shot!" He pounded Billy. "It rolled 'til it hit Santa Anna's tent. I hope that damn dictator was in it!"

Billy ran to the wall, grinning as he placed both hands on the wall, watching the huge white tent with its green silk door falling down, collapsing in green and white rolls.

A mustachioed man in his nightshirt climbed out of the tent on his hands and knees and shook his fist at the Alamo.

Sergeant Ward pounded Billy on the shoulder. "You hit him! You hit Santa Anna's tent!" he shouted as the mustachioed man jumped to his feet and ran up the hill to the west, away from Billy's cannon.

All that day and all that night, Billy was slapped and pounded on the back wherever he went.

"This here's thu Cannon Boy what hit Santa Anna's tent. Ran him out on his all-fours in his nightgown!"

Billy didn't sleep that night. Even when he went to bed, with Comanche snuggled up against his side, Billy couldn't shut his eyes. He lay on his blankets on his back, wide-eyed, reliving his glorious moment. His wonderful shot.

CHAPTER XV

The next morning Billy was nervous, too excited to stand by the quiet eighteen-pound cannon. Billy walked down the wall and turned to wave good-bye to Sergeant Ward and walked along the wall to the southwest corner of the plaza. He walked down the revetment that held the twelve-pounder at the southwest corner of the Alamo. He walked across the inner courtyard and stopped at the fire, where Cherokee Campbell was sitting next to the fire bragging on his rattlesnake belt.

"Yes, Sir, a diamond-back rattlesnake belt always brings good luck to the man what wears it." Cherokee reached down and ran his fingers under the broad rattlesnake skin belt. "It makes you so slender when trouble comes your way, that when a bullet's fired at you, it makes you twist and turn and slide away. It keeps bullets from hittin' you. I never heard of a man bein' killed while wearin' a diamond-back rattlesnake belt."

Billy took an interest in Cherokee Campbell's conversation and sat down. He reached over and felt of the diamond-back triangles in the rattlesnake skin belt. "Can a rattlesnake skin belt keep you from bein' killed by Mexican soldiers?" Billy asked.

Cherokee Campbell nodded his head. "Sure can. Ain't you ever seen bullets detour around a snakeskin belt?" Cherokee asked.

Billy shook his head. "We got lots of rattlesnakes down there on the Guadalupe River, lots of rattlesnakes and water moccasins. But I never heard that a rattlesnake skin belt would stop a bullet."

"They don't stop a bullet. They just turn 'em away."

Cherokee Campbell nodded his head. "They just make bullets detour you, sort of glide around you."

"What'll you take for that rattlesnake skin belt?" Billy asked.

Cherokee Campbell grabbed his belt with both hands and widened his brown part-Indian eyes. "My rattlesnake skin belt! It's saved my life a dozen times. I wouldn't trade it off for a sack of gold nuggets." Cherokee had a grip on his belt with both hands.

Cherokee turned his head and Billy saw him wink one eye at Johnny Hayes, who was sitting beside him at the campfire.

"I might trade you a wool blanket for that belt." Billy leaned over, touching and admiring the belt.

"Can't trade for my belt for no measly ole wool blanket." Cherokee Campbell turned his head. Billy saw him wink again at Johnny Hayes, who was across from him, on the other side of the fire.

"Don't trade him a blanket for that measly ole belt." Johnny Hayes waved away Cherokee Campbell's wink.

"I have two blankets." Billy leaned forward and ran his fingers over the outside of the rattlesnake skin belt. "I have a life I want to save. What'll you take for that belt?"

"Well I won't trade it for no wool blanket." Cherokee Campbell tightened his grip on his belt.

"Cherokee!" Johnny Hayes chided his companion. "Don't cheat that kid out of his blanket."

"Tell you what I'm gonna do, son." Cherokee Campbell turned with a gambler's gleam in his eyes. "You go over there to the horse corral and make me a horsehair reboto, a horsehair belt. I'll trade you my rattlesnake belt for your horsehair belt and a wool blanket."

Johnny Hayes held up his hand and shook his head at Billy...

Billy nodded his head quickly. "That's a trade!" he shouted. Billy jumped to his feet and started toward the horse corral. "I'm gonna climb in that horse corral right now and start shearing some mares' manes and tails. I'm gonna make a horsehair belt. How big around are you, anyway? About thirty-six inches?" Billy asked.

"Thirty-eight inches." Cherokee was on his feet. He kicked Johnny Hayes on the bottom of his boot. As Billy raced away to the horse corral, Cherokee scolded, "You keep out of this, Johnny Hayes. Let that boy make me a horsehair belt.". .

Billy spent the night shearing horses' tails and weaving the horsehairs into a belt one inch wide and forty inches long. At daybreak, he presented the horsehair belt and one wool blanket to Cherokee Campbell. He held the rattlesnake skin belt high as he walked across the plaza and up the revetment at the southwest corner of the plaza, then he held the belt behind him as he approached Sergeant Ward. He touched the Sergeant and silently he held the rattlesnake skin belt to the grizzled old cannoneer. He stood by and pressed the belt on Sergeant Ward. "I want to give you somethin'."

"Aye? What's this?" the Sergeant held up the belt, examining it.

"Would you wear this belt for me?" Billy asked.

"Whatever for?" The Sergeant felt of the scaly belt.

"It'll bring ya good luck." Billy watched as Sergeant Ward put on the belt.

Billy felt warmer when he walked back down to his bunk under the cannon along the pallisade wall. He felt warmer, even under one blanket, now that he had given the rattlesnake skin belt to the friendly old Sergeant.

CHAPTER XVI

Billy stirred in his blankets. A loud clanging noise disturbed him, and he turned and covered his head with the top of his blanket. Noises began to filter through his cover. He could hear men rising, stretching, and yawning. The sound of knives and forks and spoons clattering against dishes caused Billy to open his eyes. He heard the metal clanging again.

"Billy boy, you better roll out of there if you want any breakfast."

Billy looked up and saw Sergeant Ward standing over him, nudging Billy with his boot.

Billy threw back his blanket so suddenly that Comanche jumped to his feet with his hackles raised and his teeth bared in a protective growl. "Breakfast!" Billy shouted. "I'm hungry enough to eat leather shoe laces." Billy patted the ground beside him, motioning for Comanche to come back and sit down. "What do they feed you for breakfast in the Alamo?"

"Beef and corn." Sergeant Ward sat down beside Billy and helped him slip on his boots.

"Well, I had bacon and eggs for breakfast the other morning." Billy spoke as he slipped his boots on over his socks. "Yeah, and sweetened coffee. Don't you just love coffee sweetened with homemade syrup?"

Sergeant Ward licked his lips and shook his head. "We've been out of coffee for too many days now."

"No coffee?" Billy asked.

"This makes the seventh day since them Mexicans arrived." Sergeant Ward rose to his feet and helped Billy to his feet. "And we've got nothin' to eat but corn and beef." Sergeant Ward put his arm around Billy's back and led him toward the cook shack at the south end of the patio. "Colonel Travis warn't expectin' no Mexicans till the grass greened up in April or May, and we never laid in a supply of groceries. But we was eatin' good—bacon, ham, eggs, chicken, and even fish on Fridays till the Mexicans arrived."

Billy joined the line of unshaven men picking up plates from a table and passing in front of three cast-iron stew pots.

"What're we havin' this mornin'?" Sergeant Ward stuck his metal plate out toward Squire Daymon, the husky cook who stood behind the first stew pot with a huge fork clasped in his unwashed hand.

"You can take your pick this mornin'," Squire Daymon grinned. "Boiled beef, fried beef, or broiled beef."

"I think I'll take boiled beef this mornin'." Sergeant Ward nodded toward the center stew-pot. He nudged Billy on the shoulder. "And you better take boiled beef, too. That's the only meat in here that won't chase you to the latrine with diarrhea."

"I'll take boiled beef." Billy held his metal plate out over the center stew pot.

Squire Daymon forked a big hunk of boiled beef and dropped it on Billy's plate. He reached down into the stew pot and came up with a big beaker of gravy and poured it over the beef in Billy's plate.

Billy passed on down the line and came to a metal warming table. He held up two fingers and courtesied to the pretty lady in black curls as she set two corncakes in his plate.

"Would you like a little syrup on one of your corncakes?" the lady asked Billy.

"Yes, Ma'am, I believe I would."

The lady used a huge ladle to pour half a cup of syrup over Billy's corncakes.

Sergeant Ward pushed his plate toward the syrup barrel. "You can syrup both of my corncakes, Susannah." He nodded toward the two huge flat corncakes that covered half of his plate. "Where'd you ever find any syrup?" The Sergeant raised his plate and sniffed the sulphurous odor of the syrup.

Susannah Dickerson, the wife of cannoneer Almeron Dickerson, smiled before she answered. "My husband was in the ordnance warehouse lookin' for a barrel of gunpowder, and he picked up a barrel that was extra heavy. It turned out it wasn't gunpowder; it was syrup." Susannah laughed.

"I'd almost trade it for a barrel of gunpowder." Sergeant Ward took his fork and began forking huge mouths full of beef and syruped corncakes into his mouth as he walked to the west wall. He sat down with his back to the wall and placed his plate between his legs. "I'd almost go hungry for another barrel of gunpowder."

"We low on gunpowder?" Billy asked.

Sergeant Ward nodded his head. "We've got more gunpowder than we have shells, and we're down to a barrel and a half of gunpowder. That ain't enough to keep our fourteen guns firin' for three hours."

Billy looked across the patio to the north and saw Comanche running across the patio with his head down low as if he were about to spring on a bear. He had his hackles raised and his teeth bared as he sprung.

"Comanche!" Billy shouted as he pushed his breakfast plate aside and jumped to his feet.

Comanche dove into the air and hit a man standing in the breakfast line wearing a sombrero. The man fell to the ground and Comanche was at his throat.

"No, Comanche! No!" Billy screamed as he raced toward his dog.

Comanche had the man down and was ripping his canvas shirt, pulling it off his shoulders, jerking his striped serape cloak from side to side.

Billy dove at Comanche from the rear, grabbing him around the shoulders. Comanche turned to snap at Billy, but he softened his bite as he saw his master's hands circle his head and drop around his shoulders, pulling him to the ground.

The dark skinned Mexican was on his butt, scooting backward, away from Billy and Comanche. His dark mustache was stiff and his eyes were wide and terrified as he reached for his wide sombrero hat. He was feeling of his throat and tucking the torn pieces of his cloak back together.

"What thu hell!" Squire Daymon ran from behind his cooking pots, waving his long fork at Billy and Comanche.

Billy now had Comanche by the neck and was pulling him backward.

"Is that dog mad?" Squire Daymon asked.

Billy had pulled Comanche back to the south wall. He shook his head. "Comanche ain't mad. He's just an Indian dog, an' he don't like Mexicans."

Squire Daymon turned and looked at the Mexican who was now on his feet, still feeling of his throat and his torn shirt. "Juan Abamillo ain't no Mexican, he's a member of the garrison." Squire Daymon pointed his fork at Juan Abamillo, who had now retreated behind Squire Daymon and was staring at Billy and Comanche over Daymon's shoulder with the edges of his wide sombrero trembling.

Billy patted the ground for Comanche to sit down, and Comanche sat down. Then Billy looked up. "Comanche's an Indian dog. He don't like Mexicans. Fact is, I think he's been trained to kill 'em."

"What's this?" Colonel William Barrett Travis was racing across the patio toward the cook shack. "What happened?"

"The boy's dog nearly killed Juan Abamillo." Squire Daymon pointed his fork at Comanche, and then turned and pointed it at Juan Abamillo, who still hid behind Squire Daymon, keeping Daymon and his fork between himself and Comanche.

"Does he have rabies? Is that dog crazy?" Colonel Travis carefully stepped toward Billy and Comanche.

"No, Sir, he ain't crazy, Sir." Billy put his arms around Comanche and hugged the dog. Then he raised his head and looked at Colonel Travis. "He's been trained to fight Mexicans. He can't help himself. He just don't like people who wear sombreros and smell of garlic."

"Sombreros and garlic!" Colonel Travis put his hand to the side of his head. "My God, we've got six soldiers in here that wear sombreros and eat garlic. You'll have to tie your dog up, Billy. We can't have him runnin' around loose."

"Yes, Sir. I'll tie him up, Sir." Billy patted Comanche on the head.

Colonel Travis turned to leave. Then he turned back to Billy. "But you turn that dog loose when them Mexicans attack, you hear me?" He pointed his finger at Comanche.

As Colonel Travis walked away, Captain Juan Seguin walked slowly from the guardhouse to the cook shack with his sword drawn from his scabbard. He was holding his sword low, but it was pointed straight at Comanche and Billy.

Comanche jumped to his feet, lowered his head, raised his hackles, and bared his teeth.

Captain Seguin pointed his sharp saber at Comanche. "Is that dog crazy? Whose dog is that, anyway?" He flicked his sword and waved it at Comanche.

Comanche dove at Juan Seguin, his paws fanning the air and his teeth flashing and snapping. He struck Captain Seguin above his out-stretched arm. His flashing feet knocked the sword from Captain Seguin's hand, and his teeth bit into a red sash. In a second, he had Captain Seguin down and had pulled him away from his sword. Comanche was shaking and jerking, tightening the sash around Captain Seguin's neck.

Billy raced into the fight and grabbed Comanche by the shoulders. He put his arms around the dog's neck and pulled him away from Captain Seguin.

Captain Seguin rose to his hands and knees, shaking his head and loosening the sash that had been pulled tightly around his neck.

"Never point a gun or a sword at my dog," Billy defended Comanche.

"He nearly killed me." Captain Seguin felt of his neck. "That dog nearly killed me."

Comanche was still watching Captain Seguin, his hackles raised, his tail pointed into the air; and his ears pointed up. His eyes were following Captain Seguin. He was watching to see if the Captain was going to go for his sword again.

Billy pushed Comanche down on his haunches and commanded him to sit. He walked over and picked up the Captain's sword. He examined the blade for blood and saw none. Then he handed the sword to Captain Seguin. "I don't believe he hurt your sword, Sir."

The Captain was dusting his britches off with his glove. "He nearly choked me to death."

"Comanche don't like people in sombreros who smell of garlic."

Captain Seguin gave Billy a silent glance.

"Particularly if they're wavin' a sword at him," Billy continued.

Sergeant Ward was at Billy's side. He put one arm around Billy and led him back toward the wall. He patted Billy on the shoulder. "Your breakfast is gettin' cold."

After they sat down and were eating breakfast, Sergeant Ward reached over and ruffled Comanche's head.

"That's some dog. I don't believe he likes sombreros or garlic or red sashes. I'll bet he'll eat them Mexicans up if they ever get inside the walls of the Alamo."

Billy put his arm around Comanche, pulled him off of his feet, and snuggled Comanche's head against his. Billy whispered to Comanche quietly. "I sure don't want anything to happen to you." He raised his head and stared down at Comanche, patting the dog's head gently. "If I was the Commander of this here fort, I know what I'd do. I'd sent out for Indian dogs, 'specially Comanche Indian dogs. They sure fight." Billy shook his head, "you're gonna get in a fight an' get hurt." He grinned and rubbed Comanche's ears. "You ain't afraid of nothin', are you, boy?"

Comanche turned his dark brown eyes to Billy and wagged his tail.

"I guess not bein' afraid kinda runs in our family." Billy turned and looked at Sergeant Ward. "Sergeant, I wonder somethin'." Billy frowned and looked at Comanche. "I wonder why out of all the men that were here in the Alamo, Comanche singled out that them Mexicans and attacked them and knocked them down and tore their clothes up." Billy took a small rope from the burro cart that served as a table near the three stew pots and tied it around Comanche's neck and tied the other end of the rope to his belt.

"What'd'ya mean, son?"

"I wonder if Comanche knows somethin' about them Mexicans that you an' I don't know."

Sergeant Ward nodded his head thoughtfully. "Dogs know a lot of thinsg we don't know."

CHAPTER XVII

That night Billy snuggled under the wheels of a cannon along the pallisade joining the chapel to the north wall. He spread his blankets, wrinkling his nose as he pushed away horse manure and made his bed between the cannon wheels and the pallisade wall. He stared at the cannon barrel that jutted between the wheels and stuck out between two of the wooden posts making the pallisade wall. The cast-iron cannon barrel and the wooden wheels made Billy feel sheltered from the chill March wind.

Comanche trotted up and made a little circling survey before he laid down on the bit of blanket below Billy's feet and placed his nose between Billy's legs. He eyed Billy with the silent admiration a dog has for its master and companion. Comanche blinked his eyes a couple of times and then closed them.

Billy grinned as he felt his dog quiver and jerk in fitful sleep against his feet.

Billy was about to go to sleep when he heard the crunch of heavy boots stop and shift in the sand by the wheel of Billy's cannon.

Comanche was on his feet with his hackles and his ears raised.

"Boy, what you doin' under my cannon?"

Billy pushed back his blankets and leaned forward, patting the blanket at his feet, signaling for Comanche to lie down.

Comanche gave Billy one wag of his tail and kept his nose high and his hackles raised, studying the tall slender man with the sheepskin coat.

"I'm supposed to be sleepin' under Sergeant Ward's eighteen-pounder, but the wind's cold up there on that wall." Billy pointed toward Sergeant Ward's eighteen-pounder at the top of the revetment at the southwest corner of the fort.

"Aye. The night March wind is always cold." The tall man touched the wooden peg button at the top of his coat, raising his shoulder and pushing the sheepskin collar against his neck. "Are you one of the Gonzales boys?"

"I'm one of the men that came from Gonzales." Billy stuck out his chin.

"Oh. A man that sleeps with a dog." A grin broke across the tall man's slender, saw-sharp face.

"I'm Billy King from Gonzales. Who're you?" Billy asked.

"I'm Green B. Jamison from Kentucky, one of the many lawyers who came to San Antonio to make a stand behind these walls."

"You don't look like a lawyer." Billy looked at the man's tall leather-tonged boots, his home-spun pants, his dirty white shirt sticking out of the collar of his sheepskin jacket, and the red bandana handkerchief around his throat. "You look more like an Indian fighter than you do a lawyer."

"Right now I'm supposed to look like an engineer."

"Engineer?"

"I'm the engineer of the Alamo. I've spent the last month getting this place ready for those Mexican soldiers out there. I'm the man who designed and built this pallisade so we would have a wall between the chapel and the south wall so the Mexicans couldn't flank our south wall."

"You built this?" Billy raised his hand and patted the big wooden logs of the pallisade wall.

Green B. Jamison nodded his head. "I made the mistake of digging a well when the Mexicans cut the water off from the Alamo. My little well came in mighty handy when them Mexicans dammed up the irrigation ditch that carried water into this fort." Green Jamison placed both hands on top of the cannon wheel. "Somebody made the mistake of bragging on me, and it put me to work. I built this pallisade and I built eight revetments that allow our cannons to shoot from on top of these walls. I was an ensign in the United States Navy. I tried to build these walls and locate these cannons so each cannon can defend the other cannon with cross-fire."

"Looks like you did a good job, Mr. Jamison." Billy jerked a blanket over his head as a Mexican cannon shell lobbed over the chapel, rolled across the patio, and came to a bouncing stop against the east wall.

"Yeah, they ain't destroyed a cannon yet, and they ain't killed a man inside these walls." Green B. Jamison held on to the top of the cannon wheel and leaned backward, jerking on the wheel and studying the opposite wheel to see if his weight would raise it off the ground. "There's one thing bothers me, boy."

"What's that?" Billy asked.

"I wonder which wall they'll come over."

Billy raised from his perch against the south wall. He looked to the east, then to the north, and then to the west. Then he snuggled back against the protection of the south wall. "You think they're gonna come over one of these walls?" Billy asked.

"There's no question about them coming over the wall. I just wonder which wall they'll take."

"You think they're gonna take the Alamo?" Billy reached for Comanche, hugging his head close to his chest.

"They's a hundred and eighty-two of us, and there's four thousand of them." Green B. Jamison shook his head. "I tried to build all four walls as strong as I could. Now that it's too late to work on the walls any more, I wonder . . ."

"What's that you wonder, Mr. Jamison?" Billy asked.

"I wonder which is the weakest wall, which wall they'll take first."

"What'cha mean, Mr. Jamison?"

"It's sorta like having four fishing lines out and wondering which one the fish is going to bite first."

"Which one do you think they'll take?" Billy asked.

"Well, it's my job to see that they don't come over any wall."

"Is that why you're here, Mr. Jamison?"

Green B. Jamison nodded his head. He sighed, raised his gun and cradled it in his left arm. "Son, you ain't supposed to sleep under a cannon. Once you become a cannon boy, you're supposed to sleep in the artillerymen's quarters." He waved his arm. "Follow me." Green Jamison led the way across the patio, and guided Billy into the artillerymen's quarters along the west wall, but as he and Billy entered the low door, Green Jamison banged his head against the top of the door and cussed as he rubbed his forehead.

"Green Jamison is too tall." Johnny Ballentine spoke with his Alabama accent, from his bed on the stone floor of the artillerymen's quarters. "He just warn't made short 'nuff for these here Alamo doors. He wakes ever'body up at night cussin' when he bangs his head agin' the top o' these doors." Johnny Ballentine raised from his blanket with a grin as Green Jamison cursed and rubbed his forehead after bumping his head against the top of the door to the artillerymen's quarters. "He's taller'n most trees in Texas. He steps on trees like most men step on weeds. Bet he came from a tall tree state like North Carolina."

"Naw, he hails from Kentucky." Johnny Gaston grinned from his blankets. "We grow some mighty tall trees in Kentucky." Johnny shifted in his blankets. "Trees have to grow tall so's to find any sunlight in our rollin' hills."

"Green ain't only tall, he's a pretty fair fibber, too." Ballentine raised in his blanket and folded his hands across his knees.

"How's that?" Johnny Gaston asked.

"Green Jamison said one time he was runnin' his trap lines an' got caught in the hills after dark with nothin' but his axe, an' a bunch of wolves took after him." Ballentine continued. "Green said they warn't no trees to climb so he jest stopped an' raised one leg and them wolves jest ran around him like he was a tree." Ballentine laughed. "Green said he fooled them wolves, but one wolf raised one leg and squirted his britches leg." Ballentine blinked a big Alabama grin. "Said the damn wolf wet his leg good an' proper like 'afore he raced away with them other wolves."

"Is 'at thu truth?" Billy King asked.

"Well, you'll have to ask Green. He's thu one that says a herd o' wolves mistook him fer a tree on a dark night in Kentucky."

"I wish I was that tall," Billy gasped.

"Yeah, so do I," Johnny Gaston agreed.

The next morning the patio was chilly and foggy as the men gathered for breakfast.

"Air we gonna get anything to eat 'cept beef an' corn?" Johnny Gaston rubbed his thin belly. "I doan like beef three times a day an' I doan like goin' to bed hungry."

"That ain't beef you're eatin'," George Cottle growled from his bed on the floor.

"They ain't?"

"Nope, they's wild cattle we herded in here when the Mexicans rode up suddenly."

"Talk about wild cattle, son. I've seen 'em." George "Buffalo" Cottle pointed to his shaggy-haired buffalo jacket. "They're thicker'n trees along the San Marcos River."

"Wild cattle?" Peaceful Mitchell, a guard just coming off guard duty, blew on his corn cob pipe and blew a puff of blue smoke. "Air they free fur the takin'?"

"They're as free as a herd o' buffalo or a passel of deer." George Cottle leaned over the cast-iron stew pot.

He wiped his knife blade on his breeches leg. Then he cut a strip of boiled beef, forked it on the tip of his long-bladed hunting knife, and began eating it in huge black-toothed bites as he straightened up. "They's Partilleas cattle; cattle that turned wild when Don Felipe Partilleas abandoned his cattle and his land grant between here an' San Marcos. He was right on the road from Comanche territory to San Antonio, less than a hundred miles northeast of here." Cottle shook his head. "The Comanches raided him when they headed south toward Bexar to trade furs for whiskey and beads." He paused. "An' then Partilleas's spread came in mighty handy for the Comanches when they headed north. They robbed him coming and going. The old boy folded his tent and returned to Mexico."

"You mean the cattle are still there? They don't belong to nobody?" Peaceful asked.

Cottle nodded his head. "Thousands of wild cattle, free as the breeze."

"All you gotta do is catch 'em?" Billy asked.

"That's right." Cottle grinned a black-toothed grin between wolf-like bites. "Did ja ever try to catch a breeze?" He stomped his booted feet, laughing at wide-eyed Peaceful Mitchell, who was staring to the north, thinking of thousands of wild cattle milling around, waiting to be caught.

"Wild cattle can be caught." Billy King laid his empty breakfast plate on the floor of the cart near the fire. "When this thing's over, Peaceful, le's you and me go catch a herd of wild cows."

"I'd like that." Peaceful picked up his rifle and rubbed it thoughtfully.

"'How do ya catch wild cattle?" Galba Fuqua reached out with his city hands like he was about to grab the horns of wild cow.

"Hit takes horses, ropes, and dogs—lotsa dogs." Cottle rubbed his chin. "'Lessen you got a rifle an' jest want one for supper." Cottle reached over and lowered Galba's raised hands. "Never look at a wild longhorn cow on foot, not 'lessen you're on a horse. A good horse. Them mama cows'll fight for their calves like a bear with cubs. Even them old bulls can be mighty mean. One time they'll hiest their tails and run, an' then next time you cross their path, they'll turn and run you down. When you see a wild cow, you better be on a horse an' on a good 'un. Them wild cows got horns long 'nuff to run plum through a horse at the withers."

"My pa has caught wild horses." Billy put his hand on Peaceful Mitchell's arm and led him away from the fire. "Hit ain't so hard to do; my pa's done it twict."

"I'd sure like to get me a little spread of land an' some wild horses and a herd of wild longhorn cows. That's one reason I come to Texas. If I don't get killed, I'm gonna take me a headright of land along some pr'tty creek an' I'm gonna raise horses and cows. I want thu wild ones. They won't be nobody shootin' 'em if they're on my land." Peaceful suddenly stopped staring to the north and day-dreaming and turned to Billy King. "How did your daddy catch wild cattle?"

"I wasn't there. He said I wasn't old 'nuff, an' he didn't let me go." Billy reached for Peaceful's rifle, and Peaceful let him hold it and feel of it. "They just took dogs and extra horses and ran cattle for two days and nights and wore 'em plum out, till their tongues nearly drug the ground. Then they run 'em in a pen and kept them shut up for a week. Then when they moved 'em, they was together an' they stayed together as a herd. Pa said it takes two weeks to catch a herd o' wild cows."

"After the war, let's catch us a herd, what cha say?" Peaceful asked.

"I started to say I'd have to ask my pa." Billy grinned sheepishly. "I just forgot. I don't have to ask my pa no more."

"Mr. Mitchell, you came all the way here from Tennessee?" Billy asked Peaceful Mitchell.

"Yep."

"How'ja know there was a fort here, one that needed defendin'?"

Peaceful shook his head. "Didn't know."

"If'n you didn't know, why'dja come?"

"I was guided here." Peaceful ventured, nodding his head at the sky.

"I was wonderin' somethin'." Billy leaned back against the wall.

"What's that?"

"I wonder why any of us are here?" Billy looked up at Peaceful for an answer.

"You mean, dying?"

"Yeah," Billy leaned to his right and sniffed the powder-burned end of a broken ram-rod near the wall.

Johnny Hayes butted in from his perch near the south wall. "Texans fight for land. Tennesseeans fight for honor."

"Yeah." Peaceful's long thin face lit with a big grin. "I reckon we each fight for what we got the most of."

"I didn't come fer land, and I didn't come fer honor." Billy spoke quietly, almost to himself.

"If you didn't come fer land or honor," Peaceful cradled his rifle across his knees, "why did ja come?"

"He's got girl-trouble," Johnny Hayes laughed, "or is he old 'nuff?"

Billy shook his head and waved away Johnny Hayes's words, "I jes' came so my Pa wouldn't come." He looked at the ground between his knees and then looked up.

"That's honor." Johnny Hayes nodded his head as he spoke.

CHAPTER XVIII

Grey haired Robert McGregor carried his bag down to the well dug by Green Jamison. He took his knife and began cutting and trimming his 51-year-old hair and began humming and quietly singing a Scottish song.
"Ye take the high road
an' I'll take the low road
an' I'll be in Scotland
A'fore you"

Billy came down to the well and watched the old man trim his hair and take a "dry bath," using a bucket of water and a wash cloth, washing parts of his body as he changed into clothes he took from his travel bag.

"What's that?" Billy walked around the old Scotchman as he flipped and dusted off a scotch plaid skirt and stepped into it and pulled it around his waist and buckled it with a leather belt.

"Tis me uniform," Robert McGregor spoke quietly, almost to himself. "When a Scotchman dies, he dies with honor." The grey-topped Scotchman sat an odd-shaped red cap over his head and pressed it into shape. "An' a Scotchman always wears his uniform if he ha'e one." He dusted off a red and white checked blouse and put it on. He raised one arm and smelled of the wool blouse. "A Scotchman always takes a bit o' Scotland with him so he won't be in a lonely foreign land when he's laid tae his final resting place." The Scotchman now put on white shoes and green leggin-socks. Then he bent over as he reached and dug into his heavy leather bag and brought out a leather and cloth instrument of bright colors.

"What's that?" Billy asked as he watched the Scotchman carefully fondle the gadget and spread it across his shoulders.

"Tis a Scottish bagpipe."

"A what?" Billy asked as he eyed the Scotchman in a skirt.

Robert McGregor touched his fingers to three leather bags that reminded Billy of cows' udders. McGregor pulled in a huge lungful of air and touched his lips to a black piccolo-like instrument and puffed up his bagpipes. He raised his head high in the air and marched to the center of the patio blowing and playing his Scottish bagpipe.

Billy listened to the strange tingling music and watched the proud man wearing a plaid skirt instead of pants. Billy shut his eyes and put both fingers to his ears to soften the shrill whine of the bagpipe.

Suddenly the sound filled the Alamo, and floated out beyond.

Cannonading from the Mexican side of the San Antoinio River stopped.

"Them Mexicans stopped shooting at us!" Galba Fuqua shouted from his perch atop the west wall. "Their cannons have gone silent!"

The only sound in the Alamo was the lonely wail of Robert McGregor's bagpipe. When its awesome wail crossed the San Antonio River the Mexican soldiers and cannoneers quit shooting and turned their heads and listened.

In the silence from across the river, there flowed a reverence, a respect that could be felt as well as heard.

The Mexican Generals knew a Scotchman was wearing his kilts in the Alamo. They had heard how the kilted Scotch fought at Waterloo—fierce demons in skirts who fought bitterly, to the last man, inspired by high fluted bagpipes.

Mexican General Fisola, who had been at the Battle of

Waterloo with Napoleon's Italian troops, shook his head.

"Have Scotchmen come to the aid of the Alamo?" He shook his feathered hat. "Mountaineers from Tennessee and Kentucky, that's bad enough, but do we have to fight Scotchmen too?" He shouted to Colonel Almonte who spoke excellent English as they stood side by side on the west side of the river, eyeing the Alamo solemnly.

Courtesy
Daughters of the
Republic of Texas Library,
San Antonio, Texas

CHAPTER XIX

After Robert McGregor's bag-pipe serenade, the Mexican cannons remained silent for a few minutes. Then they cannonaded again, more furiously than ever, concentrating their fire on the south wall. The cannons busted a hole in the south wall. Cannonading stopped. At dark on Billy's fourth day in the Alamo, the Mexican guns fell silent.

Billy left Comanche tied to Sergeant Ward's eighteen-pound cannon and climbed down to the patio and went by the cook house at the north end of the patio and filled his hat full of shelled corn. He carried it folded under his arm to the stockade near the chapel, where the horses were kept. He climbed the split rail fence and made his way slowly and quietly to Alexander. Billy pressed his head against Alexander's neck and hugged him. The old horse nudged him and shook his mane, telling Billy how glad he was to see him. Then he smelled the corn in Billy's hat. He snorted happily while Billy stood in front of the horse holding his hat under Alexander's nose where he could eat the corn and nod his head to his heart's satisfaction.

"They say we won't be needin' any corn after tomorrow." Billy held the hat full of corn in one hand and used the other hand to push the hair out of Alexander's eyes. "I thought if we wouldn't be needin' any corn, at least I knew an ole horse that's been on mighty short rations for four days now." Billy turned around and held the corn in front of him and pressed his back against Alexander's front haunches, leaning against his horse while Alexander filled his belly full of shelled corn. Billy leaned his head against his horse's neck and petted him with his free hand.

"You like this quiet, this silence from the cannon fire, don't you, ole horse? It's about dark an' a good time to sleep and rest. Makes you think of home, don't it, Alexander?" Billy blinked his eyes. A bit of moisture wet the corner of Billy's eye and dripped down on his cheek and ran to the bottom of his chin. It shook there for a moment before Billy wiped it away on the sleeve of his coat. "You can go home, Alexander. I'm gonna take you to the horse gate and turn you loose, and I want you to go home and tell Mama . . . an' Papa an' . . ." Another tear blinked in the corner of Billy's eye. "I want you to tell 'em about me an' the Alamo. Tell Mama I sent you home 'cause you weren't needed. Tell her I said there weren't no way for you to help fight Mexicans, an' I sent you home to help put in a spring garden." Billy pressed his head against his horse's neck as the tears ran down his cheeks. He dropped his hat on the ground and turned and put both arms around his horse's neck and sobbed. "Tell Pa that I did the right thing. Tell him that we died here so that a family can live in quiet happiness away from cannon fire." Billy leaned against his horse with his arms clasped tightly around Alexander's neck until the tears stopped coming. He stepped back and patted the horse gently, picked up his hat and poured the few grains of corn that were left on the ground, and put his hat on the back of his head. Billy put his hands on his hips and smiled at his horse. "There's one other thing I want you to do, Alexander." He grinned sheepishly at his horse. "I want you to stop by the Anderson place." Billy's grin grew. "I know you ain't much at huggin' an' kissin', but I want you to knock at Amy Anderson's door and when she comes out, if you can't give her a hug and kiss, at least give her a good nudge with your nose. Will you do that for me?" Billy smiled at his horse as Alexander nodded his head and wiggled his mane. "You tell her hello for me, and if she ever wants a ride, you give her a good ride, you hear now?"

Billy took a halter off the corral fence and put it over Alexander's head. He led him out the corral gate to the inner patio. He led him across the inner patio to the gate at the northeast corner of the Alamo. Billy stopped at the gate and led Alexander by the rope halter to the door that opened to the outside world.

"Where you takin' your horse, Billy boy?" Henry Warnell, the gate-keeper for the day, stepped forward with his rifle.

"I'm gonna turn my horse loose. I want him to go home an' help Ma an' Pa work the land and give a message to my mama."

"Don't you think you'd better turn your horse over to them Mexicans." Henry Warnell walked around Alexander, examining him and frowning. As he studied Alexander's bony sides and knotty shanks, Henry Warnell shook his head. "Poorest excuse for a horse I ever saw. He couldn't out-run a hobbled mule," Henry laughed. "An' they ain't 'nuff fat on him to make two bars of soap. Them Mexicans'll take one look at that skinny horse an' walk away." The short ex-jockey from Arkansas shook his head. "Them Mexicans won't bother that horse none; you can bet on that. Don't believe the Mexicans would have him if you gave 'im to 'em."

"That's why Alexander'll get home. Nobody much would want him." Billy looked at the ground for a moment, then looked up. "But my mama and papa'll appreciate him."

"How'd'ya know he'll go home?" Warnell reached down and loosened the steel bolts on the door. He cracked the door open a couple of inches and peered through the crack out into the dark outside world.

"Ole Alexander's smarter'n most people. He'll stand around outside the gate for a while, and when I don't come on out, he'll start headin' for home. He'll get there quicker than I could."

Henry Warnell opened the door. Then he stepped into the doorway. "Ain't you gonna tie a letter on him or nothin'?"

"I told him, I told him what to do."

"Oh?" Henry Warnell looked at Billy, then at Alexander. He opened the door. "Oh. I didn't know." He held the door open.

Billy lifted the halter and led Alexander out the door. He put his arms around Alexander's neck and hugged and kissed him. "You go home an' kiss Ma an' Pa for me." Billy walked back through the door. After the door was closed, Billy stood waiting and listening until he heard Alexander's hoofs pound away toward the southeast.

Billy held both arms high against the gate, shutting and tightening his eyes, squeezing them shut.

Henry Warnell lowered his rifle, setting it on the ground against his boot, leaning against the long barrel. He blinked as he watched the boy's long arms reach the door and quiver. The arms came down slowly and slumped limply by the boy's side. Billy stared up into the night sky as Henry Warnell raised his arm and wiped away a sniff. He stepped aside as Billy turned and walked slowly across the star-lit patio. At the north wall, Billy stared at the night sky. "Now if there was just some way to save Comanche." He headed toward Comanche tied to the wheel of Sergeant Ward's big cannon.

CHAPTER XX

At dusk on the fifth of March, after a big hole had been breeched in the south wall, the cannonading from the Mexicans in San Antonio stopped suddenly. They had done their job; they had a hole in the wall. An ominous silence rose in the fort. Sergeant Ward was suddenly sober. He rose from his gun mounts on the eighteen-pounder at the southwest corner of the Alamo. He raised his powder smeared head high in the air and cupped his blackened hand over his good ear. "What's that I hear?"

Cherokee Campbell from Tennessee put on his Indian grin. "That's silence you hear."

"You sure that's silence?" Sergeant Ward asked, raising his head higher in the air and turning his ear. "Sounds awful, don't it?"

Cherokee Campbell didn't say anything. He just grinned at the godly, peaceful silence, enjoying it for the first time in eleven days.

"I thought I had lost my hearing; I thought I was stone deaf." Sergeant Ward rubbed his ears and listened again. "I never thought silence sounded like that." He shook his head. "Sounds sort of scarey."

Cherokee Campbell stared at the blackened wiping cloth. "Even wild animals tremble with fear in silence. I've seen deer tremble and shake just before I shot 'em."

"Maybe we're deer just fixing to get shot." Sergeant Ward leaned on his ramrod.

Peaceful Mitchell lowered the butt of his rifle to the ground and stared over the west wall toward San Antonio. He could hear a rooster crowing in a chicken coop across the San Antonio River. "Did you hear that rooster crow?" Peaceful asked Sergeant Ward.

Sergeant Ward nodded.

"That proves you ain't deaf." Peaceful grinned.

Sergeant Ward nodded again.

"Don't that rooster crowing sound odd after all the cannoneering and rifle shots and bugle calls in the middle of the night? Imagine hearing a rooster after all that racket."

"Maybe they're fixing to leave; maybe they're fixing to move out," Galba Fuqua grinned.

"They won't leave now. They've busted a hole in the south wall." Cherokee Campbell squinted in the darkening twilight, trying to make out the hole blasted in the south wall near the artillerymen's quarters. "They might have left if we had got reinforcements from Goliad. But they know what we know. Fannin ain't comin'."

The silence was broken by a strong voice coming from the inner patio. "This is Colonel Travis. I want all able-bodied men not needed for guard duty to assemble in the patio." Peaceful stared at Sergeant Ward, and then at Cherokee Campbell. "I'm a guard." Peaceful bit his lip. "I'll have to stay on guard duty."

"I imagine we're going to prayer meeting," Sergeant Ward growled and wiped his hands on the wiping cloth. He started down the gun parapet toward the inner patio.

Cherokee Campbell started to lay his rifle down against the wall, but he thought better of it and put it over his shoulder. He followed Sergeant Ward down the parapet.

Billy started walking down the wall, snuffing the pure air, suddenly cleansed of the sulphur smoke of gunpowder. Peaceful Mitchell stopped his marching along the north wall and sat down and leaned back against the wall when he saw Colonel Travis mount a barrel. A candle lit the patio. Billy stood beside Sergeant Ward near the front of the soldiers inside the patio that circled Colonel Travis' barrel.

"I have a few words, Gentlemen," Colonel Travis began with his arms outstretched, like a preacher pleading at the end of his sermon. "I know this is March and you have not been paid since last October. I am fortunate to have even one man. I have deceived you." Travis had his head raised high in the air, and it looked like his eyes were closed. "I have kept your spirits high with the hope that we would be relieved by Fannin's garrison at Goliad. I deceived not only you, but myself, too, for I believed Fannin would come. Jim Bonham has just now returned from Goliad with word that Fannin is not coming to the relief of the Alamo. Now I know the truth, and the truth is that he is not coming. We stand alone, and we will not be relieved. We are now faced with a decision." Travis lowered his arms. His sigh of pain could be heard throughout the Alamo. "Only two choices face us. We can stand and fight, or we can run. I'm going to ask you to vote on which action we are to take. Before you vote, I must tell you this. I was sent here by Governor Smith with specific instructions to destroy the Alamo. I must also tell you that Colonel Bowie was sent here by General Houston with instructions to destroy the Alamo. We did not carry out our instructions. We walked around these walls and we grew strength from the sturdiness of these stone walls. We elected to stay and fight. We ask no man to stay with us whose heart tells him to do otherwise." Travis drew his sword and held it high in the night air. "I shall draw a line in the sand of this holy patio, and I shall step across that line. I ask that those who wish to stand and fight with me step across that line with me, and all those who do not step across will be free to leave. I pray that God will guide you in your decision." Travis stepped down from the barrel and walked sharply to the west, to the west wall. He stuck his sword in the ground and walked eastward, scratching a line in the sand with his sword as he marched. He stopped and placed his sword back in his scabbard and stepped across the line to the north, leaving all of his men on the south side of the line. Travis stood stiffly, eyeing his men. "Those who wish to stand and fight may join me by stepping across this line." He pulled his sword out and pointed at the line.

"There's 4,000 Mexican troups out there and there's only 183 of us Texans. When they attack in force, we know what is going to happen. We will lose. We will all die. But it is possible to win even in losing. If we fight like Tennesseans and Alabamans and Scotchmen and Texans always fight, and fight long enough and hard enough, we can make this such an expensive victory that Santa Anna's army may win here, but be unable to win another battle in Texas. This is what I ask you to fight for. I ask you to stand with me and die in such a way that we win victory in death."

Billy saw a stirring in the lines of men as they looked about for guidance. Then Davy Crockett shouldered his rifle and stepped across the line, followed by his twelve Tennessee Mounted Volunteers. Suddenly the whole line moved, until only two figures remained on the south side. Billy saw James Bowie lying on his cot on the south side of the line. Bowie raised up on one elbow. "Colonel, I can't walk across that line. I'd be much obliged if you'd have some boys move me across." Billy watched four men step back across the line and lift Bowie's cot. Little Joe Bayliss, Robert Campbell, another Tennessean, Squire Daymon, and the old chicken thief, Johnny Hayes, each had a corner of Bowie's cot. They carried him across the line and set him down gently and stepped away.

Bowie raised on his cot and looked back across the line at the only figure that still stood immobile on the south side of the line. Everybody stared at Luis Moses Rose.

"You seem not ready to die with us, Rosie boy." Bowie's voice was strong and clear, not accusative.

"No, I am not ready to die." Rose leaned on his rifle "Moses Rose had already died once. I died in the retreat of Napoleon's Army from Moscow. God let me live through that. I live by retreat. I didn't come to Texas to die; I came to Texas to live."

"Even if you escape, Rosie boy, even if you get over the wall, you'll be caught," Bowie argued.

"Not me," Rose felt of his dark hair. "I speak Spanish and I have dark hair and dark skin. Moses Rose could pass as a Mexican even before Santa Anna himself." Rose stood beside his rifle, remaining on the south side of the line.

"I don't know whether I wish you luck or not." Bowie turned his back to Moses Rose.

Rose laid down his rifle and stared at it for a second. He straightened up and wiped the sand off his hands, then walked to the west, around the line. He went into the artillerymen's quarters. He came out with a pack of clothes. He climbed the escarpment to the wall and dropped his packet of clothes on the other side. Rose dropped over the wall and disappeared into the night.

The assembly in the patio remained still and motionless, watching Rose climb over the wall and disappear into the night. Until he dropped his clothes over the wall, Billy didn't think he would really leave. As Luis Moses Rose disappeared over the side of the wall, Billy felt an urge to see someone raise their rifle and shoot. He wondered what emotion made him want Moses Rose shot. Was it cowardice or was it courage? Billy wondered.

CHAPTER XXI

Billy was attracted by two low fat candles lighting the bed of the burro cart that was packed near Jim Bowie's room near the north gate. Men were standing around the flat bed of the burro cart, writing on yellow paper with turkey feather quills, dipping them in charcoal ink, filling the bottom of a broken whiskey jug, set on its side at the rough edge of the cart.

"What're they doing?" Billy whispered to Galba Fuqua.

"Writin' wills."

"What's a will?" Billy asked.

Galba shrugged. "A will's a paper you sign in front of two witnesses, sayin' what ya want done with your land an' things when you're gone."

"Oh!" Billy watched two men carry Jim Bowie out to the burro cart on his cot. "That's Jim Bowie!" Billy gasped. "Is he writin' his will?"

"Reckon so." Galba looked down, shuffled the patio sand with his booted foot, leaning over, examining his little toe, sticking out the side of his ragged boot. "Wish I had something to leave somebody in a will."

"Yeah. I hear Jim Bowie owns a million acres of land. I bet his will is longer'n a Bible." Billy and Galba laughed.

"I ain't got nothin' left but Comanche." Billy sighed and felt of Comanche's tufted ears. "I done sent my horse, Alexander, home to help Ma and Pa put in a turnip patch."

"You had a horse o' your own?" Galba moved closer to Billy.

Billy nodded.

"An' you got Comanche too." Galba sighed. He

looked down at his ragged boots with his toes sticking out the cracks in his boots. "All I got is a worn out pair o' boots."

"Yeah, I got Comanche." Billy grinned at his dog.

"You gonna make a will an' leave Comanche to somebody?"

Billy shook his head. "They ain't nobody I'd leave Comanche to."

Galba stood wide-eyed, staring into Billy's blue eyes. "You wouldn't leave Comanche to me?" Galba touched his chest.

"Oh, I never thought 'bout somebody wantin' Comanche."

Galba pointed to his own chest. "I wish somebody'd mention me in a will." He shifted his feet. "I ain't never had no horse, 'er no dog, no nothin'." He looked at his boots. "Just a pair o' worn out boots."

Billy slapped Galba on the shoulder. "You leave me your boots an' I'll leave you ole Comanche."

"Yeah. Let's make a will, then maybe I'll have something, even if it's after . . ." Galba's voice trailed off.

"Everybody in the Texas Army gets 320 acres of land, that's part of our pay." Billy slapped Galba. "You're nearly as rich as Jim Bowie."

"Yeah." Galba grinned. "If I knew who my Mama and Papa were, I could leave them 320 acres of land."

"You know somethin'," Billy studied Galba in the dim candlelight, "if we was to live through this war we'd have 640 acres. We could work together an' own cows and go down on the desert an' catch wild horses and stock us a ranch an' we'd be the richest kids in Texas."

"Yeah, that'd be fun. Wish we wasn't gonna die tomorrow." Galba studied the west wall, standing between him and the Mexicans.

"Yeah, it'd be fun. Mama'd like that." Billy's face turned red.

"You even got a mama to cry for you." Galba blinked.

CHAPTER XXII

"Lieutenant Dickerson got promoted to Captain." Sergeant Ward climbed up the revetment and stared over the wall at the Mexican lines.

"He did, did he?" Billy asked.

Sergeant Ward nodded his head. "Colonel Travis asked whose cannon it was that shot down General Santa Anna's tent, and when he was informed that it was Lieutenant Dickerson's cannon, the Colonel slapped his hand against the hilt of his sword and promoted him to Captain."

"Oh?" Billy looked down at the stone revetment. Then he raised his head and grinned at Sergeant Ward. "It was his cannon, wasn't it?"

"Yeah, it was his cannon, alright." Sergeant Ward kicked a cannon wheel. "But you aimed it and you fired it." Sergeant Ward shifted his cud of tobacco and squirted a black arc of tobacco juice over the stone wall.

"You loaded it, Sergeant." Billy tugged on Sergeant Ward's black coat. "Maybe He'll promote you to Lieutenant."

"Naw, I don't want no promotion." Sergeant Ward rubbed his beard. "Wouldn't take it if they gave it to me. What good would a promotion do? We ain't been paid since last October."

"Sergeant, you mean nobody in this fort's been paid?" Billy asked.

Sergeant Ward shook his head. "It's been more'n four months since any of us was paid."

"Oh, I didn't know that." Billy shrugged his shoulders.

"I don't care nothin' about no promotion." Sergeant

Ward continued bending over his cannon, rubbing the barrel with a cloth. "The only good a promotion will do anybody in this fort will be to change the prefix on their tombstone. The only good it will do Dickerson is when they bury him, it'll be Captain instead of Lieutenant."

"You think so, Sergeant?" Billy asked.

Sergeant Ward tightened his jaw as he looked at Billy. "They keep shootin' at us night an' day, an' we can't fire back. We ain't got enough powder and shells. The only time we can shoot is when they're attacking the fort with dragoons and bayonetted infantrymen. It don't matter how many men you kill, they got more men than we got shells." Sergeant Ward pounded his fist on the wall. "Dammit, they should've made a Captain out of you instead of Dickerson."

Billy rubbed Sergeant Ward. "I wouldn't want to be ranked higher than you, Sergeant Ward."

Sergeant Ward unfolded his oiled cloth and popped it at Billy's foot. "Fightin' with the likes of you, Billy Boy, makes me job a little more bearable."

It was almost daylight on March 6, 1836. Major Baugh was making his rounds, checking the guards, raising his lantern as he stepped over each sleeping figure.

"Corporal of the Guard, post number eight. Who's on duty?" Major Baugh raised his lantern.

"Cherokee Campbell, Sir. Post number eight all clear and quiet. Not a sound."

"It's awful quiet out there, ain't it?" Major Baugh commented.

"Quiet like the stillness just before a thunderbolt." Campbell pulled his blanket around his shoulder and shifted his rifle from his left hand to his right hand. He warmed his left hand against his shirt.

"Is that Billy?" Major Baugh raised his lantern and pointed at Billy King huddled in his blanket with his arm around the shoulders of his dog, Comanche.

"Yeah," Sergeant Ward grinned at his cannon boy.

"He came up here in the night and sat down beside me. He put his hand in mine and we talked. Didn't say much; mostly talked with our eyes. He's worried about me, and he's worried about his dog. He's 'fraid the Mexicans'll kill Comanche."

"They probably will." Major Baugh lowered his lantern and leaned over, looking at Billy huddled with his arm around Comanche. "That Comanche's a fightin' dog. He sho' hates Mexicans." Major Baugh sighed and raised his lantern high, trying to see through the darkness beyond the Alamo walls. "Well, I've made my rounds. I find it all quiet on the Alamo walls. I guess I'd better go make my report."

A rifle cracked from the darkness outside the walls. Major Baugh dropped the lantern and grunted as he reached for his head. He staggered two steps. The roar of cannon fire belched toward the four walls of the Alamo and dulled the sound of Major Baugh's thudding fall from the wall.

Rifles cracked, bugles blew, drums rolled, cannons fired, muskets rattled, and screams rent the first break of day. Horses' hoofs by the hundreds clattered on the hardened clay outside the walls.

Captain Dickerson licked his lips and blew a shrill whistle that broke the stillness inside the Alamo. "An attack on the west wall!" he shouted.

"An attack on the south wall!" Wash Cottle shouted.

"They's a thousand damned Mexicans storming up this here east wall!" Johnny Balentine's Alabama drawl announced the attack.

"Wake up, you Tennessee Volunteers!" Davy Crockett shouted from the pallisade as he squinted one eye and fired at the on-coming wall of Mexicans.

Billy threw aside his blanket and ran to his post at the eighteen-pound cannon. Billy raced westward down the wall toward the fuses and match sticks. Billy grabbed a fistful and raced to the eighteen-pound cannon.

Sergeant Ward was whistling an Irish melody as he lowered the muzzle of the eighteen-pounder as daylight crept in from the east.

Billy felt a bullet whiz by his cheek. He watched as Sergeant Ward leaned over the cannon, still whistling, aiming down the barrel.

Sergeant Ward stepped back and pounded the wedge in deeper, lowering the muzzle of the cannon still lower. Sergeant Ward stopped whistling and shut his aiming eye. "Light that match fuse! They're comin' by the thousands!" Sergeant Ward shouted.

Billy lit the match fuse and held it above his head and looked at Sergeant Ward. When Sergeant Ward nodded his head, Billy touched the match fuse to the fuse hole. The cannon belched in a mighty roar and jumped backward. Billy winced as he saw the grape shot made of broken horse shoes ram into the line of charging Mexicans, shredding them into bloody dust.

Comanche raised his nose to the sky and howled. Then he tucked his tail between his legs and ran down the wall, looking for a place to jump down off the wall at the charging Mexicans.

The screams and yells echoed against the walls. Comanche's hackles were raised. The hair stood up on his back between his shoulders. With his tail between his legs, he ran back down the wall to crawl between Billy's legs. He looked up at Billy for help, for comfort and protection from the sceams and shouts and cries and the roar of cannons and the whistle of bullets.

Billy reached over and patted Comanche on the head between the ears while the eighteen-pounder was being scraped clean of spent gunpowder. The Scotsman, McGregor swamped her out while Sergeant Ward held his hand over the fire hole.

Bullets and cannon shells were whistling by and chipping limestone splinters off the wall. Billy heard a rifle fire not far to his left. He turned and saw Squire Daymon, the cook, lower his rifle and blow smoke out of the barrel.

Billy grinned as he stepped forward to touch his match stick to the vent hole, and he stumbled over Comanche, who was curled up in shivering, trembling paralysis at Billy's feet.

The fire of cannons was constant. Comanche was shaking and trembling like a wounded buffalo.

"Somebody shoot that dog and get him out of our way!" McGregor, the Scottsman, cursed. "Damned cowardly cur!"

"No! Don't shoot my dog! Don't shoot Comanche!" Billy leaned over and protected his dog with his arms and his shoulders. He looked up at Sergeant Ward. "Comanche's a' Indian dog. He ain't used to all that cannon fire and all this screamin' and hollerin' an' all this smell of gunpowder."

"You sponge the cannon," Sergeant Ward ordered. Then he grinned at Billy. "That dog'll give them Mexicans fits when they get close enough for him to use his teeth."

The Mexican charge broke after the sixth shot of the eighteen-pounder. It shredded the charging line of bright-uniformed Mexican soldiers with their crossed shoulder straps.

Two ladders had been set against the wall and were shaking and trembling as Mexicans tried to climb to the top of the wall.

Billy picked up a ramrod and raced forward, pushing the ramrod against the top of the ladder, pushing it away from the wall. He could feel the weight of men on the ladder as he pushed. He heard the curses and the screams and the shouts as the men on the ladder rolled backward and fell to the ground.

Billy ran down the wall and used the ramrod to push another ladder away from the wall, spilling the Mexican soldiers onto the ground.

Billy grinned as he raised his ramrod in the air triumphantly. "Ramrods are good for some things besides ramming cannons!" he shouted as he raced back for the eighteen-pounder.

"Good boy." Sergeant Ward patted Billy on the back. He stepped forward and leaned over the wall, staring into the twilight. "We broke 'em! Look at 'em run!" Sergeant Ward pounded one hand against the top of the wall. "They're runnin' for the river! They're runnin' for cover!" He turned and looked at Billy with a grin on his face, which darkened into a frown. "If we just had a cavalry to keep 'em runnin', we'd have this battle won."

"How we doin'?" Billy ran down the wall toward Captain Dickerson and his twelve-pound cannon. He patted him on the back as he turned to watch the Mexicans stumbling and falling in their mad rush to get away from the withering fire coming from the Alamo.

"We gave 'em a lickin', Billy Boy. We gave 'em another lickin'." The Captain grinned as he watched the Mexican soldiers running away from the Alamo. Then the Captain frowned as he witnessed swords flashing behind the line of retreating Mexicans soldiers.

"Santa Anna's got his cavalry out to stop his soldiers from runnin' all the way to Mexico," Captain Dickerson laughed.

"We whupped 'em, didn't we? We really whupped 'em."

"We whupped 'em that round, but the day's not over, yet." Captain Dickerson watched the Mexican cavalry stop the retreat of the black-hatted Mexican infantrymen and turn them back toward the Alamo. "It might be a long day."

"What'sa matter, Comanche?" Billy held Comanche's muzzle between his hands and stared into his eyzs. "You tucked your tail between your legs and ran like a . . ." Billy looked over the wall at the Mexicans. "You ran like a cowardly Mexican."

Comanche's ears were straight and alert. His nose was twitching and sniffing the air that was now becoming clear of gunpowder smoke.

Billy patted Comanche on the head. He stood up and walked away from the dog, shaking his head, talking to himself. "I never knew Comanche was no coward."

Sergeant Ward heard Billy's words. He grabbed him as he walked by and turned him around, holding him by his shoulders. "That dog's no coward." Sergeant Ward looked at Comanche. "He's afraid of guns and cannons; all animals are. If them Mexicans ever get within range of his teeth, you watch him; he'll fight."

"I don't know, Sergeant." Billy shook his head.

"Well, I do. This battle ain't over. We ain't got to the rough and tumble yet. We've just seen the first round. You wait'll them Mexicans get in the walls. That dog'll kill as many Mexicans as Crockett." Sergeant Ward smiled.

Billy looked up at Sergeant Ward. "You think they'll get in?"

Sergeant Ward nodded his head. He leaned over and patted Comanche. "And when they do, ole Comanche'll make us look like a bunch o' cowards."

Billy got down on his knees and ruffled Comanche's ears. "He won't be a member of the King family 'less he does his share of the fightin'."

Billy ran back to Sergeant Ward and the eighteen-pound cannon. "Sergeant Ward, you keep that rattlesnake belt buckled on real tight, now. Don't you let anything happen to that belt."

The old Sergeant nodded at his cannon boy as he began reloading his cannon. He surveyed the Mexican infantrymen running toward the walls of the Alamo with the cavalry behind.

"They're comin' again!" Galba Fuqua shouted as he bit on the bullet clamped between his teeth and spat it down the barrel of his rifle.

A cold wind blew in from the north, wafting the gunpowder away. Sergeant Ward raised straight up, then raced for the wall. He leaned over the wall, staring toward the west, where the Mexican soldiers were reassembling near the San Antonio River.

"What's goin' on out there?" Sergeant Ward shouted.

McGregor leaned over the wall beside Sergeant Ward. "Aye, they're turnin' away. They're not comin' toward our eighteen-pounder." The Scottsman grinned through his gray beard.

"My God!" Sergeant Ward pounded the top of the wall with both fists. "There's a breech in the north wall! They're all headed toward Colonel Travis's post!" Sergeant Ward stepped back and surveyed the stream of thousands of Mexicans running for the north wall. "Unbuckle that cannon an' turn her around! We're gonna have to fill that breech with dead Mexican soldiers!" Sergeant Ward shouted as he grabbed a wheel and began turning the eighteen-pounder around so it would fire at the hole in the north wall, which was quickly being filled with bayonetted Mexican soldiers. They were firing their rifles and bayonetting their way into the inner patio.

"Uh," Sergeant Ward grunted through clenched teeth as he bent over, grabbing his belly with both hands. White sweat broke out on his powder-blackened face. He staggered to his knees, holding his belly, watching the blood seep through his fingers. "Keep that cannon firing." He shut his eyes and bent over, shuddering.

McGregor bent over Sergeant Ward for a second before he toppled backward. His eyes rolled as blood gushed from a neat hole in the top of his head. He trembled and shook for a moment, and then lay still.

Comanche jumped to his feet. Hair rose on his back, and his tail was stiff as he studied the Mexicans streaming into the Alamo. His hackles were high as he raced down the revetment toward the first line of Mexican soldiers streaming into the Alamo.

One Mexican came at him with a bayonet. Comanche jumped aside. His teeth flashed as he grabbed the Mexican's leggings and sent him sprawling to the ground. He was at the Mexican's throat, ripping and shredding. Then he raised his head and dove at a Mexican whose back was to him, carrying him to the ground, gnashing and slashing at his neck and throat.

Three Mexicans started after Comanche with their bayonets. He side-stepped the first thrust and dove, bringing the white-sashed Mexican officer to the ground. He was ripping the Mexican's throat when two bayonets slashed into his side. He disappeared into the reeling turmoil of bodies, men, and gunpowder.

Comanche had stopped the advance long enough for Billy to fire the eighteen-pounder. When the smoke cleared, Billy looked for Comanche, but he couldn't see anything but bones, legs, and bloody uniforms. Then he heard a scream to his left and saw Galba Fuqua topple to his knees and roll like a dropped cannon ball.

Courtesy
Daughters of the
Republic of Texas Library,
San Antonio, Texas

CHAPTER XXIII

Billy jerked as a bullet chipped the stone near his chin. He felt a burn near his ear. He reached up and pulled a chip of stone out of the bottom of his ear. There was blood on his fingertips. Galba Fuqua lay on the ground, now, kicking his feet. "They don't even let a soldier say good-bye to his friends." Billy jumped to his feet and waved good-bye to Galba Fuqua. He raced back to Sergeant Ward and the eighteen-pounder.

"They've breeched the north wall!" someone shouted, pointing to the stream of black-headed Mexican soldiers pouring through the shattered wall. "We'd better turn this cannon around and aim at that hole in the wall and stop them before they take this fort. Grab a spike, Billy Boy, and we'll lift this trail and turn it around."

"Aye, Mr. Warnell; I'll lend a hand." Billy leaned over and suddenly felt the weight of the three coats that he was wearing. In the cold before dawn he had donned Thomas Hendricks' buffalo skin vest. Then when it kept on getting colder, Lieutenant Dickerson had noticed him shaking and had loaned him one of his two great coats. The extra coats were warm, but they were cumbersome and made it difficult for Billy to lean over and then straighten up.

"Dig in with your spikes, boys. We're shootin' downhill." Henry Warnell ducked a bullet that bounced off the cannon barrel as he aimed at the hole in the north wall. His head jerked as the sparks flew. "Got me in the eye." Warnell spat to wash away the blood trickling from his seared eye. "Take the match stick and fire the piece!"

Warnell handed the powder match to Billy. "They got me good eye; I can't see."

Billy took the match stick and touched it to the vent hole, and the eighteen-pounder roared, firing bits of chain and pieces of horseshoe at the men streaming through the breeched north wall.

"We got about twenty, sir."

Sergeant Ward nodded his head from his bloody position near the cannon wheel. Then he raised his arm. "Spike the piece back into position. Swab her out." Sergeant Ward was shouting orders faster than Billy and Henry Warnell could carry them out.

"The bore is clean, and she's sponged."

"Charge the piece!" Sergeant Ward grabbed his chest.

Billy looked down at the Sergeant as he rammed in the powder.

Sergeant Ward grabbed Billy's ankle as Billy rammed in a load of broken chain and horseshoes.

"We ain't got time for no grommet, Sergeant."

"Keep her firin', Billy Boy." Sergeant Ward patted Billy's foot.

Billy charged the vent hole with powder and lifted the match stick to the vent hole.

"Boom!" The cannon roared.

Billy looked down and saw that Sergeant Ward was dead.

"The rattlesnake-skin belt didn't work." Billy leaned over Sergeant Ward's bleeding body, tears streaming down his face.

"The belt works." Cherokee Campbell dodged an incoming cannon shell. "The protection of the belt belongs to the owner, not necessarily the man who wears it, but the one who has earned the totem, the snake's protection."

"But Sergeant Ward's dead."

"That means someone else wears the totem. Somebody else has the protection."

A bullet tore through Billy's shoulder, twisting him around. He saw Henry Warnell grab his stomach and stumble backward. Another bullet tore through Billy's great coat. Bullets were hitting Billy, but they were hitting his coats, not hitting him, tearing through his coats and jerking and turning him in sharp jerks as they hit and tore through his outer coats. He was now alone. Bullets were whistling right and left. Billy blinked against a shower of dust as the bullets ricocheted off the stone walls. To the north, Billy saw men still pouring through the hole in the north wall. Tears streamed down his face from the dust in his eyes as he sponged out the cannon and charged it with a powder bag. Billy pulled the ramrod out and grabbed a double hand full of broken horseshoes. He stuffed them into the cannon and rammed them in snugly against the powder. Bullets were now tearing into his coat and twisting his leg. Billy glanced around the walls of the Alamo as he charged the vent hole with powder and raised the powder match. He saw no other men standing around the walls. Was he alone?

He touched the powder match to the vent hole and the huge cannon fired, ripping into the horde of men streaming into the inner patio.

Billy could hear the Mexicans shouting and running. As he sponged out the eighteen-pounder and re-loaded it, eight Mexicans, their bayonetts flashing in the early light, raced up the revetment toward Billy. Billy charged the vent hole and lowered the cannon barrel with a wedge. He touched the powder match to the vent hole just as the Mexicans got to the muzzle of the eighteen-pounder. The cannon jerked, and as it blasted, Billy saw mincemeat pieces of Mexicans flying through the air down the revetment.

Billy was busy hopping to the sponge bucket. Bullets were whistling and ricocheting, jerking and turning him.

"That boy on the wall!" English-speaking Colonel Almonte of the Mexican Army waved his sword at Billy. "Can't anybody hit that boy on the wall?"

Bullets battered Billy as he raised his ramrod and pushed powder into the cannon. The bullets were hitting his clothes, twisting and turning him, but the bullets were missing his body.

A hot pain tore into Billy's shoulder as a bullet knocked the ramrod out of his hand and sent him to the ground.

Billy heard a Mexican standing over him say, "Un hombre bravo. A brave man."

Courtesy
Daughters of the
Republic of Texas Library,
San Antonio, Texas

CHAPTER XXIV

Billy lay on his back. He felt blood trickling out of his left leg just below the hip. He felt a numbness in his right shoulder where a bayonet had cut through to the bone. His boot had been blown off his left foot. One of his fingers was powder-burned, but he wasn't dead.

A Mexican officer in a high plumed hat stood over Billy, leaning over, studying him with his hands placed behind his back. He wore a green jacket and a white silk shirt. His hair was neatly trimmed, and he had the look of an aristocratic officer.

Billy heard the Mexican officer say, "Muchacho." He shook his head. Then the officer spoke English, "Only a boy."

Billy was squinting through one half-shut eye, but now he opened both eyes and stared at the tall, handsome officer standing over him.

"El muchacho, el muchacho." A Mexican soldier pointed his bayonet at Billy. "No muerte." Blood was dripping off of the tip of the soldier's bayonet.

"He is not dead!" The green-jacketed officer pushed the soldier away. "I am Colonel Juan Almonte. We thought you were dead."

"I am bleeding to death." Billy grimmaced as he attempted to move his right arm. It wculdn't move.

"Un hombre bravo." The Mexican soldier with the bloody bayonet tipped Billy's chin as he lowered the bayonet to Billy's throat. He put both hands on the handle of his rifle as he prepared to ram the bayonet into Billy's throat.

"No!" The green-jacketed officer shoved the soldier

away. "He is just a boy."

The Mexican soldier stepped back, fingering his leather chin strap, and began shouting as he pointed and shook his fist at the piles of dead and mangled Mexican soldiers at the foot of the revetment to Billy's cannon.

Billy raised his head just a bit. He was now on the patio floor. He remembered being carried there on the bayonet of a Mexican rifle that had pierced his shoulder. He raised up on one arm, and through the Mexican legs that surrounded him, he could see the match fuse still in Major Evans' hand, where he had run toward the ordnance room and its gunpowder. Billy remembered the wounded look Sergeant Ward had suffered when Colonel Travis had ordered Major Evans to blow up the powder house. Billy saw that the Major never reached the powder house. His fuse lay on the floor of the patio. He wondered if he could get up and grab the powder match and get to the powder house with it. He grinned. Sergeant Ward would like that.

Yeah, he could blow up the Alamo while it was full of Mexicans!

Billy moved his head, looking through the Mexican legs at the smouldering match fuse still in Major Evans' hand. If he could reach that match fuse and run fifteen yards and drop it in the gunpowder in the ordnance room ... If he could just get to his feet. He tried to raise his leg, but it wouldn't move. He reached down and touched it, and brought his hand away covered with blood. His leg felt like something dead. He licked his lips. He had one arm and one leg. Was there any way he could reach that match fuse? He glanced around him, looking for a rifle or a stick, or even a sword, that he could use as a crutch. The men of the Alamo were dead. They wouldn't mind if the fort were now blown up.

Billy saw Galba Fuqua's body being picked up and carried on four bayonets by four Mexican soldiers, his arms and legs flopping in the grotesque stiffness of death. Then four Mexican soldiers grinned as they rammed their bayonets into the body of Major Evans. They carried him away, his head hanging low and his arms and legs kicking and wobbling, bouncing on the bloody ground. Billy saw Sergeant Ward's huge body being carried on top of four cross rifles. They were dumping the bodies in a pile in the center of the Alamo patio.

Billy saw the legs of Mexican soldiers step aside. He saw the white legs of an officer followed by a large group of green-jacketed officers in silk and satin.

"What have we here?" The officer in the silk white britches stopped and stared at Billy.

"It is a boy, Mr. President." Colonel Juan Almonte nodded his head at Billy, who remained half raised on one elbow.

"A boy you say?" General Santa Anna leaned forward and glanced down at Billy with a frown across his dark forty-year-old visage. "He is not dead!" General Santa Anna looked at Colonel Almonte.

"He is only a boy." Colonel Almonte pointed his finger at Billy's unshaven chin.

"But he fought like a man! He fought like a hundred men!" The Mexican soldier with the bloody bayonet pointed the bloody rifle at Billy.

"You say he fought?" General Santa Anna asked the soldier with the bloody bayonet.

"Si, he killed these men. He killed all of these men." The soldier pointed at the pile of bodies below the revetment to Billy's cannon.

"A brave man." Colonel Almonte folded his arms across his chest, blinking his eyes at Billy with admiration.

"Then let him die like a man!" General Santa Anna shouted, waving his arm at Billy.

"You are going to kill the boy?" Colonel Almonte turned to General Santa Anna.

"Si. He will die anyway." General Santa Anna pointed

his white leather boot at Billy's bloody leg. "We flung the duello. The drums played the duello of no quarter. We flew the black flag of no quarter." General Santa Anna turned and looked at Billy with a bitterness around his lips. "They asked no quarter from us, and we will give them none. Bayonet him to death." General Santa Anna turned and walked away.

The Mexican soldier with the bloody bayonet raised his rifle high and shoved his bayonet into Billy's stomach with a grin.

Billy gritted his teeth. "I wonder if Sergeant Ward would be proud of me."

Billy's body was carried to the funeral pyre and placed at the top of the pile of defenders of the Alamo. His slender young body was placed beside those of Jim Bowie and David Crockett, and when the Mexican soldiers burned the carcasses at 11:00 a.m. on March 6, 1836, a Mexican soldier carried the torn body of an Indian dog and tossed it on the pile with his young master.

THE END

General Santa Anna won the Battle of the Alamo, but his victory was so costly his troups were defeated by General Sam Houston with 783 men at the Battle of San Jacinto at 3:00 p.m. April 21, 1836.

The Cannon Boy of the Alamo did not die in vain. Nor did his dog, Comanche.

There are boys like Billy and dogs like Comanche wandering the hills and valleys of Texas even today. They will never die.

Canyon Public Library

Templeton, Lee
Cannon Boy of the Alamo

T
B
K52

23,315

DATE DUE

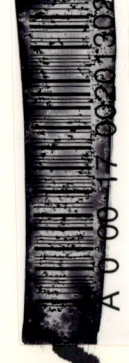